MARIAN GETZ SPENT HER CHILDHOOD AS THE DAUGHTER OF MISSIONARIES IN THE CONGO, AFRICA. SHE LEARNED HOW TO COOK BY READING HER MOTHER'S COOKBOOKS AND USING A CAST IRON WOOD BURNING STOVE. SHE OWNED HER OWN CATERING COMPANY IN KANSAS BEFORE BECOMING THE DISTRICT TRAINER FOR CAKE DECORATORS OF A MAJOR FLORIDA GROCERY STORE. A PASTRY CHEF FOR WOLFGANG PUCK SINCE 1998, MARIAN HAS BEEN FEATURED IN SEVERAL NATIONAL MAGAZINES AND WAS SELECTED BY HER PEERS AS ONE OF THE TOP 10 CHEFS IN CENTRAL FLORIDA. SHE HAS ALSO BEEN HONORED WITH THE "OUTSTANDING ACHIEVEMENT AWARD" IN 2007 FROM HER ALMA MATER, OTTAWA UNIVERSITY. MARIAN HAS TAKEN HER EXPERIENCE AS A PASTRY CHEF, WIFE, MOTHER, AND NOW GRANDMOTHER TO PUT TOGETHER A PRESSURE COOKER COOKBOOK THAT WILL NOT ONLY SATISFY ALL YOUR CULINARY NEEDS, BUT ALSO HELP YOU BECOME A BETTER CHEF IN THE KITCHEN. THIS COLLECTION OF AMAZING RECIPES, MOUTH WATERING PHOTOS, MARIAN'S HELPFUL TIPS AND RESOURCE PAGE WILL HELP YOU MAKE EFFORTLESS HOMEMADE FOOD IN THE PRESSURE COOKER FOR THE ENTIRE FAMILY.

A most sincere thank you to our wonderful viewers and customers for without you there would be no need for a cookbook. I try very hard to give you an array of recipes suited for the particular kitchen tool the cookbook is written for. Wolfgang and I create recipes faster than we can write them down. That is what chefs do and is also the reason to tune in to the live shows and even record them so you can learn new dishes that may not be in our cookbooks yet.

Thank you most of all to Wolfgang. You are the most passionate chef I know and it has been a privilege to work for you since 1998. You are a great leader and friend. Your restaurants are full of cooks and staff that have been with you for 20 or more years which is a true testament to how you lead us. Thanks for allowing me to write these cookbooks and for letting me share the stage at HSN with you.

To Greg, my sweet husband since 1983. Working together is a dream and I love you. You have taught me what a treasure it is to have a home filled with people to laugh with.

To my sons, Jordan and Ben, we have a beautiful life, don't we? It just keeps on getting better since we added Lindsay, J. J., precious Easton and our second grand baby Sadie Lynn.

To all the great people at WP Productions, Syd, Arnie, Mike, Phoebe, Michael, Nicolle, Tracy, Genevieve, Gina, Nancy, Sylvain and the rest of the team, you are all

amazing to work with. Watching all the wonderful items we sell develop from idea to final product on live television is an awe-inspiring process to see and I love that I get to be a part of it.

To Daniel Koren, our patient editor and photographer, thank you for your dedication. You make the photo shoot days fun and you are such an easygoing person to work with in the cramped, hot studio we have to share. We have learned so much together and have far more to learn.

To Greg, Cat, Estela, Angi, J.J., Laurie and Margarita who are the most dedicated, loving staff anyone could wish for. You are the true heroes behind the scenes. You are a well-oiled machine of very hard working people who pull off the live shows at HSN. It is a magical production to watch, from the first box unpacked, to the thousands of eggs cracked and beaten to running to get that "thing" Wolf asks for at the last minute, to the very last dish washed and put away it is quite a sight to behold. I love you all and I deeply love what we do.

Today's generation of pressure cookers are designed to ensure safe and easy cooking. This appliance uses steam pressure to break down the fibers of the food allowing for faster cooking times. Tough meats become tender quickly, vegetables and grains are infused with flavors, and foods retain their nutrients. Although the pressure cooker is mainly used as a timesaving device, it works for fine cooking as well.

When I asked Marian to write the cookbook for the pressure cooker, I knew she would rise to the occasion. Her experience as a pastry chef, wife, mother, and now grandmother allowed Marian to put together a pressure cooker cookbook with a wide variety of recipes that I'm sure you will use for years to come.

A student of cooking is probably one of the best ways to describe Marian. She is always looking for something new, something fresh, something local, something seasonal. Her culinary knowledge combined with her passion for cooking is second to none. The recipes that Marian has written for this cookbook will motivate you to be more creative in the kitchen.

As I learned long ago, alongside my mother and grandmother, you should always put lots of love into everything you cook. This is certainly evident in this cookbook.

Wolfgang Puck

FAVORITES

BEGINNINGS & SIDES

ENTREES

TABLE OF CONTENTS

TABLE OF CONTENTS

PRESSURE COOKING TIPS

Cooking food in your pressure cooker is one of the best time and money-saving methods in the kitchen. Pressure cooking can be up 70% faster than regular cooking and can save up to 70% energy compared to traditional cooking. Foods cooked under pressure have a wonderful flavor as the food gets infused with flavor. As a result, less salt, herbs and spices are necessary which also saves money since herbs and spices can be expensive. In addition, pressure cooking retains more nutrients and essential vitamins in the food. What's not to love about pressure cooking?

MEATS

If you like fall-apart, tender, juicy meats cooked in less than an hour, then the pressure cooker will become a dear friend in your kitchen. The pressure cooker is able to achieve such tender meats in a short time by cooking in a sealed and pressurized environment which causes the temperature inside to rise considerably higher than the normal simmering temperature of 212°F. This is great news for busy cooks who just want to make hassle-free meals that taste good.

VEGETABLES

If you are a vegetarian or vegan, or your doctor is encouraging you to eat more vegetables, then there is no finer way to cook such foods than using a pressure cooker. I pressure cook dried beans as well as dark, leafy greens at least 5 times a week and do it in minutes instead of hours thanks to my pressure cooker. Also, pressure cooked foods retain more vitamins and nutrients than foods cooked on the stove top or oven because they are cooked far more rapidly and in considerably less liquids.

COOK ONCE – EAT TWICE

You will love having a larger size pressure cooker, even if you are just cooking for 1 or 2 people. Pressure cooked foods taste even better the next day and freeze beautifully. Divide your cooked food into portions then store in the refrigerator or freezer. This is a great way to have several meals just waiting for a too-busy-to-cook day. Any time you can cook once and eat twice you are saving your precious time as well as money.

LIQUID

The pressure cooker requires the use of liquid to operate properly. The liquid creates steam which builds up and raises the temperature which is the reason it cooks so fast. If you don't add enough liquid or your liquid is really thick, for example using BBQ sauce by itself, there will not be enough liquid to build steam and the pressure cooker will switch to warm mode. If this happens, carefully remove the lid and adjust the liquid accordingly. If you want to try your own recipe creations in the pressure cooker, use this rule of thumb to estimate the liquid needed: Add 1 cup of liquid (water, broth, wine etc.) then add 1/3 cup liquid for every 15 minutes of cooking time.

FROZEN FOOD

If you are adding frozen items to the pressure cooker, you do not need to adjust the cooking time specified in the recipe. The pressure cooker can only come to pressure once the contents boil, so it will take a bit longer to reach pressure but the cooking time should remain the same.

RELEASING PRESSURE/STEAM NATURALLY

In most cases, especially when pressure cooking meats, it is important to allow the pressure inside the unit to release naturally after cooking (this takes about 10 minutes). The reason this is so important is that when meat cooks under pressure, the fibers open up and become soft and tender. If you quickly release the pressure manually, the sudden rush of cold air inside the pressure cooker causes those same fibers to tighten up rapidly which will toughen the meat. Please allow the pressure to release naturally after cooking for the most tender food. I like to unplug the pressure cooker after cooking is complete then set my kitchen timer to 10 minutes before carefully opening the pressure cooker and serving the delicious food.

RELEASING PRESSURE/STEAM MANUALLY

Some recipes in this book call for the pressure to be released manually. Certain foods such as vegetables do not benefit from natural steam release like meats do so releasing the steam manually helps speed things up. To release pressure manually, unplug the pressure cooker and turn the steam vent to **VENT**. Use caution when manually releasing the pressure as hot steam will be released. Use tongs or a kitchen towel to turn the steam vent.

OVERFILLING

The pressure cooker will not work if you overfill it. There must be enough empty space inside the pressure cooker for the pressure to build. If you overfill the unit, the food will boil instead of cooking under pressure.

HISSING NOISE

If your pressure cooker makes a hissing noise, you may not have the seal valve seated correctly. Use a pair of tongs or a kitchen towel to gently nudge the valve which should stop the hiss. The hissing noise it makes when adjusting the valve is normal. It should make a soft hissing sound but not a loud one and there should not be a steady stream of steam escaping. If you do see this it is usually due to overfilling the pressure cooker. Sometimes it is caused by the gasket that is pinched or crooked so it cannot form a proper seal. Clean the gasket and lid after every use. See the user manual for more information.

CANNING

This pressure cooker is not suitable for canning. Even though this pressure cooker seems large enough, there is not enough interior head-space for proper canning pressure to build.

ALUMINUM FOIL SLING

If you are baking in the pressure cooker, it can be difficult to add or remove the baking vessel, such as a baking dish, from the pressure cooker. You can fashion a "sling" out of a piece of aluminum foil to help you move the cooking vessel in and out of the pressure cooker. Once you place it in the pressure cooker, tuck the excess foil inside the pressure cooker. Once done cooking, simply lift the foil sling out of the pressure cooker by the handle.

STEP 1:
Use a strip of aluminum foil about 20-inches long.

STEP 2:
Fold the aluminum foil strip in half lengthwise.

STEP 3:
Bring the two ends together then fold the ends tightly to make a "handle".

STEP 4:
Place cooking vessel inside the center of the sling.

SE CAUTION

is very important to always use caution when using the pressure cooker as the steam and condensation an be very hot. Always use a pot holder or kitchen towel when handling the lid, pressure cooker insert or il sling. Remember to unplug the appliance before removing the pressure cooker insert.

ALT

he salt used in this book is Diamond Crystal Kosher Salt. It is half as salty as most other brands. This is ecause the grains are very fluffy and therefore not as many fit into a measuring spoon. This brand also ts only "salt" as the ingredient in the box. If you are using a different brand than Diamond Crystal Kosher alt, simply use half the amount specified in the recipe. If you are following a reduced salt diet you may mit or reduce the salt called for but of course the taste will be different.

ANILLA

adore vanilla and order both my vanilla extract and vanilla beans from a supplier directly from the island f Tahiti. Tahitian beans and extract are my favorite. I use both of these in recipes where the vanilla takes enter stage in flavor. If vanilla is not the star flavor, I use imitation vanilla. It adds the correct taste and roma without overpowering the stronger flavors in the recipe and is far less expensive. I am also crazy bout an inexpensive imitation flavoring called Magic Line Butter Vanilla Extract. It adds an incredible weet smell and taste to baked goods. Its aroma reminds me of how a really good bakery smells.

CHOCOLATE

Buy good quality chocolate and cocoa. It is easy to find excellent chocolate at most grocery stores but it is almost impossible to find good cocoa powder. If you can't find it locally, please see the source page 106 for my favorite place to buy online.

BUTTER

All of the butter used in this book is unsalted. Softened butter means butter that has been left at room temperature for several hours. It should be soft enough to offer no resistance whatsoever when sliced with a knife. While there is no substitute for butter's pure flavor, you can use a substitute such as margarine if necessary. Most of the recipes will turn out fairly well.

SWEETENER

If you need to use a sugar substitute, my favorite kind is an all-natural product called Zsweet. I get it at my local health food store. While it does not bake as perfectly as regular sugar, it is the best substitute I know. My other choice is stevia. I also really like agave syrup and use it in many of my recipes if a liquid form of sugar can be used.

9

PANTRY TIPS

Being prepared to cook the recipes in this book, or any recipe for that matter, is one of the keys to success in the kitchen. Your pantry must be stocked with the basics. We all know how frustrating it can be when you go to the cupboard and what you need is not there. This list includes some of the ingredients you will find in this book and some that I try to keep on hand.

IN MY PANTRY:

Olive oils
Canola oil
Kosher salt
Black pepper in a mill to grind fresh
Chicken flavored bouillon powder, such as Maggi
Beef flavored bouillon powder, such as Maggi
Vegetable flavored bouillon powder, such as Maggi
Cayenne pepper
Variety of dried spices
Garlic, fresh and granulated
Onion, fresh and granulated
Vinegar, white, apple cider and balsamic
Worcestershire sauce
Sriracha hot sauce
Soy sauce and liquid aminos

Honey
Variety of sugars
Sweeteners such as Stevia and Zsweet
Ketchup
Mustard, dried, yellow and grainy
Mayonnaise
Variety of pickles
Pepperoncini
Chipotle chiles in adobo sauce
Variety of dry beans
Variety of pasta
Variety of rice
Canned foods such as tomatoes, tuna,
green chiles, tomato paste, pasta sauce, soups

IN MY REFRIGERATOR:

Carrots
Celery
Garlic
Ginger
Lemons
Limes
Cabbage
Dark, leafy greens

Lettuce
Mushrooms
Parmesan cheese
Basil, cilantro, sage and green onions
Eggs
Butter
Apples and citrus
Milk and almond milk

IN MY FREEZER:

Garlic ginger starter
Pesto
Ground beef
Chicken
Peas
Broccoli
Raspberries
Spinach
Dark, leafy greens like collards, turnip greens

ON MY COUNTER:

Bananas
Onions
White potatoes
Squashes
Garlic bulbs
Tomatoes

It is not necessary to have all the items listed at all times. However, if you are feeling creative, adventurous or just following a recipe, it's great to have a good selection in the kitchen.

CORNED BEEF & CABBAGE

Makes 4-6 servings

Ingredients:

1 corned beef brisket (3 pounds), flat cut
1 tablespoon mixed pickling spices, wrapped in cheesecloth
1 small white onion, sliced
2 1/3 cups water or beer
2 large carrots, peeled and chunked
1 pound small red bliss potatoes, halved
1 small green cabbage head, cut in wedges
Grainy mustard, for serving

Method:

1. Place the corned beef, pickling spices, onions and water or beer into the pressure cooker; secure lid.
2. Set steam vent to **SEAL** and timer to 60 minutes.
3. When cooking is complete, let pressure release naturally (about 10 minutes).
4. Carefully transfer the beef to a cutting board and cover.
5. Add the carrots, potatoes and cabbage to the pressure cooker; secure lid.
6. Set steam vent to **SEAL** and reset timer to 5 minutes.
7. When cooking is complete, carefully release the pressure manually (see tips on page 7) then remove lid.
8. Slice the beef across the grain then transfer to a serving platter.
9. Transfer the vegetables from the pressure cooker to the platter then serve with grainy mustard.

GRANDMA'S HEARTY BEEF STEW

Makes 4-5 servings

Ingredients:

tablespoons canola oil
tablespoons cornstarch
osher salt and fresh pepper to taste
pound beef chuck, cut into 1-inch cubes
cups beef stock
/4 cup store-bought ketchup
tablespoon Worcestershire sauce
teaspoons soy sauce
bay leaf
medium white onions, cubed
garlic cloves, minced
Russet potatoes, cubed
carrots, diced
celery stalks, chopped

Method:

1. Set timer to 20 minutes and let pressure cooker preheat for 5 minutes with the lid off.
2. Add the oil to the pressure cooker.
3. Sprinkle the cornstarch, salt and pepper over the beef then turn to coat.
4. When oil is hot, add half of the beef to the pressure cooker and cook until browned on all sides; remove then repeat with remaining beef.
5. Return all of the beef to the pressure cooker then add remaining ingredients; stir then secure lid.
6. Set steam vent to **SEAL** and reset timer to 12 minutes.
7. When cooking is complete, let pressure release naturally (about 10 minutes).
8. Discard the bay leaf, adjust seasoning if desired and serve hot.

MIGHTY
MAC & CHEESE

Makes 6 servings

Ingredients:

3 1/2 cups elbow or other small pasta, uncooked
2 cups chicken stock
1 can (12 ounces) evaporated milk
1 tablespoon unsalted butter
1 teaspoon dry mustard
Pinch of cayenne pepper
1 teaspoon kosher salt, or to taste
1 tablespoon store-bought ketchup
15 American cheese slices
4 ounces extra sharp Cheddar cheese, shredded
2 ounces Monterey Jack cheese, shredded

Method:

1. *Place all ingredients, except Cheddar and Monterey Jack cheeses, into the pressure cooker; secure lid.*
2. *Set steam vent to **SEAL** and timer to 6 minutes.*
3. *When cooking is complete, carefully release the pressure manually (see tips on page 7) then remove lid.*
4. *Add remaining cheeses and stir until melted before serving.*

OLD FASHIONED
POT ROAST

Makes 4-6 servings

Ingredients:

pounds beef chuck
small potatoes, scrubbed and halved
teaspoons minute tapioca
large yellow onion, peeled and chopped
cups baby carrots
celery stalk, sliced
bay leaf
garlic cloves, sliced
1/2 cup store-bought ketchup
tablespoon powdered beef bouillon, such as Maggi
3/4 cups water
Kosher salt and fresh pepper to taste

Method:

1. *Place all ingredients into the pressure cooker; secure lid.*
2. *Set steam vent to **SEAL** and timer to 40 minutes.*
3. *When cooking is complete, let pressure release naturally (about 10 minutes).*
4. *Garnish as desired and serve hot.*

TIP

For thicker gravy, remove meat from pressure cooker after cooking then reset timer to 5 minutes. Dissolve 2 tablespoons cornstarch in 1/3 cup cold water and add to the boiling liquid. Whisk until thickened and bubbly then serve over the pot roast.

EASY BEEF STROGANOFF

Makes 4-6 servings

Ingredients:

1 tablespoon unsalted butter
1 pound ground beef
1/2 medium yellow onion, diced
2 celery stalks, diced
2 garlic cloves, minced
4 ounces button mushrooms, sliced
1/2 cup chicken stock
1 cup evaporated milk
Kosher salt and fresh pepper to taste
Hot buttered noodles, cooked
Sour cream, for garnish

Method:

1. Set timer to 20 minutes and let pressure cooker preheat for 5 minutes with the lid off.
2. Add the butter to the pressure cooker.
3. When butter sizzles, add the ground beef; stir using a wooden spoon to brown the beef.
4. Add the onions, celery and garlic then cook for 3 minutes or until onions are tender.
5. Add remaining ingredients, except sour cream and noodles; secure lid.
6. Set steam vent to **SEAL** and reset timer to 7 minutes.
7. When cooking is complete, let pressure release naturally (about 10 minutes).
8. Taste and adjust seasoning if desired then serve over noodles with a dollop of sour cream.

EASY CHICKEN ENCHILADA CASSEROLE

Makes 4-6 servings

For the Casserole:

can (15.5 ounces) dark red kidney beans, drained and rinsed
can (15.5 ounces) yellow corn
jar (17.35 ounces) enchilada sauce
can (6 ounces) diced green chiles
package (1.12 ounces) taco seasoning mix
cups chicken stock
0 whole frozen chicken tenders
large yellow onion, diced
red bell pepper, diced

For Finishing:

cups tortilla chips
cup Monterrey Jack cheese, shredded
cilantro
jalapeño peppers
our cream
green onions

Method:

1. Place all casserole ingredients into the pressure cooker; stir then secure lid.
2. Set steam vent to **SEAL** and timer to 15 minutes.
3. When cooking is complete, let pressure release naturally (about 10 minutes).
4. Add tortilla chips and cheese then serve with desired accompaniments.

EASY GLAZED MEATLOAF

Makes 4-6 servings

For the Meatloaf:
3 white bread slices, cubed
1/3 cup whole milk
1 pound lean ground beef
1/2 pound ground pork
4 bacon slices, finely chopped
1 large yellow onion, chopped
2 garlic cloves, minced
2 large eggs, beaten
1 teaspoon kosher salt
1/2 teaspoon fresh pepper
1/3 cup store-bought ketchup
1 tablespoon store-bought yellow mustard
1 tablespoon store-bought Worcestershire sauce
1 1/2 cups water
Parsley for garnishing

For the Glaze:
1/4 cup store-bought yellow mustard
1/3 cup store-bought ketchup
1 cup light brown sugar, packed

Method:
1. In a large bowl, combine all meatloaf ingredients, except water and parsley; mix gently together.
2. Apply nonstick cooking spray to a 7-inch baking pan that will fit inside the pressure cooker.
3. Press the meatloaf mixture into the pan then smooth the top.
4. Place a metal rack into the bottom of the pressure cooker.
5. Make a foil sling for the baking pan (see page 8).
6. Pour the water into the pressure cooker then lower the baking pan into the pressure cooker using the foil sling; secure lid.
7. Set steam vent to **SEAL** and timer to 30 minutes.
8. When cooking is complete, let pressure release naturally (about 10 minutes).
9. Remove lid then remove baking pan by the foil sling.
10. Combine all glaze ingredients in a saucepan; simmer over medium heat until thick and shiny.
11. Top meatloaf with glaze, garnish with parsley, cut into slices and serve.

SWISS STEAK

Makes 4 servings

Ingredients:

1 tablespoon canola oil
4 pieces cube steak (2 pounds total)
1 large yellow onion, peeled and sliced
2 large carrots, peeled and cut into 1/4-inch coins
2 tablespoons red wine vinegar
1 cup beef stock
1 bay leaf
2 celery stalks, trimmed and cut into 1/4-inch pieces
8 very small red potatoes
3 tablespoons tomato paste
Kosher salt and fresh pepper to taste

Method:

1. Set timer to 20 minutes and let pressure cooker preheat for 5 minutes with the lid off.
2. Add the oil to the pressure cooker.
3. When oil is hot, add 2 steak pieces to the pressure cooker and brown lightly on both sides then remove and repeat with remaining steak pieces.
4. Place all steak pieces and remaining ingredients into the pressure cooker; secure lid.
5. Set steam vent to **SEAL** and reset timer to 30 minutes.
6. When cooking is complete, let pressure release naturally (about 10 minutes).
7. Taste and adjust seasoning if desired and serve.

BOURBON CHICKEN

Makes 4 servings

Ingredients:

2 tablespoon canola oil
2 pounds boneless, skinless chicken, cut into 1-inch pieces
1 garlic clove, crushed
1/4 teaspoon ginger
3/4 teaspoon crushed red pepper flakes
1/4 cup apple juice
1/3 cup light brown sugar
2 tablespoons ketchup
1 tablespoon cider vinegar
1/2 cup water
1/3 cup soy sauce
1 tablespoon bourbon (optional)

Method:

1. Set timer to 20 minutes and let pressure cooker preheat for 5 minutes with the lid off.
2. Add the oil to the pressure cooker.
3. When oil is hot, add the chicken pieces and cook until browned.
4. Combine remaining ingredients in a large mixing bowl.
5. Pour mixture into the pressure cooker then stir to coat the chicken; secure lid.
6. Set steam vent to **SEAL** and timer to 8 minutes.
7. When cooking is complete, let pressure release naturally (about 10 minutes).
8. Serve immediately.

TIP

I like to serve the bourbon chicken with rice and steamed cabbage.

IN A HURRY CHICKEN CASSEROLE

Makes 6 servings

Ingredients:

- chicken thighs or breasts, with or without bones
- cups elbow macaroni, uncooked
- cups water
- cup half & half
- 1/2 tablespoons powdered chicken bouillon, such as Maggi
- medium yellow onion, diced
- tablespoon dried sage
- /4 teaspoon cayenne pepper
- teaspoon apple cider vinegar
- Kosher salt and fresh pepper to taste
- cup saltine crackers, crushed

Method:

1. Place all ingredients, except saltine crackers, into the pressure cooker; secure lid.
2. Set steam vent to **SEAL** and timer to 20 minutes.
3. When cooking is complete, let pressure release naturally (about 10 minutes).
4. Sprinkle saltine cracker crumbs over the casserole, garnish as desired and serve.

BBQ BEEF BRISKET
DINNER

Makes 6-8 servings

Ingredients:

3 pounds beef brisket, trimmed
2 large carrots, chopped
2 large yellow onions, quartered
2 celery stalks, chopped
1 tablespoon powdered beef bouillon, such as Maggi
1 1/2 cups ginger ale or water
1/2 cup store-bought ketchup
1 cup bottled BBQ sauce
Kosher salt and fresh black pepper to taste

Method:

1. Layer all ingredients in the order listed above into the pressure cooker; do not stir and secure lid.
2. Set steam vent to **SEAL** and timer to 60 minutes.
3. When cooking is complete, let pressure release naturally (about 10 minutes).
4. Garnish as desired and serve hot.

TUNA CASSEROLE

Makes 4 -6 servings

Ingredients:

2 cups long-grain white rice, uncooked
2 cans (5 ounces each) tuna, drained
1 large yellow onion, chopped
2 celery stalks, chopped
1 cup chicken stock
3/4 cup whole milk
10 ounces frozen peas
Kosher salt and fresh pepper to taste
1 cup Cheddar cheese, shredded
2 ounces cream cheese, softened

Method:

1. Place all ingredients, except cheeses, into the pressure cooker; stir then secure lid.
2. Set steam vent to **SEAL** and timer to 6 minutes.
3. When cooking is complete, let pressure release naturally (about 10 minutes).
4. Gently stir in both cheeses.
5. Taste and adjust seasoning if desired before serving.

SHREDDED PORK TACOS

Makes 6-8 servings

For the Pork:

4 pounds pork shoulder
8 garlic cloves, minced
1 large white onion, sliced
2 tablespoons powdered pork or chicken bouillon, such as Maggi
Kosher salt and fresh pepper to taste
2 teaspoons ground cumin
1 teaspoon oregano
1/2 cup whole milk
1 cup water

For Serving:

Corn or flour tortillas
Green cabbage or lettuce, shredded
Favorite cheese, shredded
Fresh or store-bought salsa
Purple onion slices
Cilantro, chopped
Avocado slices
Lime wedges

Method:

1. *Place all pork ingredients into the pressure cooker; secure lid.*
2. *Set steam vent to **SEAL** and timer to 35 minutes.*
3. *When cooking is complete, let pressure release naturally (about 10 minutes).*
4. *Remove pork then skim excess fat from the surface of the liquid in the pressure cooker.*
5. *Use a pair of tongs and a fork to shred the pork into thin, long pieces.*
6. *Return pork to the liquid inside the pressure cooker; stir well then adjust seasoning if desired.*
7. *Serve with tortillas and desired toppings.*

BBQ
PORK CHOPS

Makes 4 servings

Ingredients:

1/2 cup all purpose flour
1 teaspoon cayenne pepper
Kosher salt and fresh pepper to taste
4 pork chops (3/4-inch thick)
1 tablespoon canola oil
1 cup bottled BBQ sauce
1 1/3 cups chicken stock

Method:

1. In a plastic bag, combine the flour, cayenne pepper, salt and pepper; close bag and shake well.
2. Add the pork chops to the plastic bag then shake until pork chops are coated.
3. Set timer to 20 minutes and let pressure cooker preheat for 5 minutes with the lid off.
4. Add the oil to the pressure cooker.
5. When oil is hot, add 2 pork chops and brown on both sides; remove and repeat with remaining chops.
6. Place all pork chops, BBQ sauce and stock into the pressure cooker; secure lid.
7. Set steam vent to **SEAL** and reset timer to 20 minutes.
8. When cooking is complete, let pressure release naturally (about 10 minutes).
9. Serve with additional BBQ sauce if desired.

CHEESY TURKEY TETRAZZINI

Makes 4-6 servings

Ingredients:
- cups spaghetti, uncooked
- cups chicken stock
- pound turkey, cooked and chopped
- tablespoons unsalted butter
- ounces button mushrooms, sliced
- cup mozzarella cheese, shredded
- /4 cup Parmesan cheese, grated
- cup Greek yogurt
- /2 cup frozen peas, thawed
- Kosher salt and fresh pepper to taste
- cup cheese crackers, crumbled

Method:
1. Break the spaghetti into thirds then place the spaghetti, stock, turkey, butter and mushrooms into the pressure cooker; secure lid.
2. Set steam vent to **SEAL** and timer to 5 minutes.
3. When cooking is complete, let pressure release naturally (about 10 minutes).
4. Gently stir in the cheeses, yogurt and peas; stir until cheeses are melted.
5. Taste and adjust seasoning as desired.
6. Serve with crumbled cheese cracker on top.

TIP
You can substitute the turkey with any leftover meat that you might have in the refrigerator. Leftover pot roast, pork roast or rotisserie chicken work very well. For a crunchy topping, scatter a handful of canned French fried onion rings over each serving.

GRANDMA'S MEATBALLS

Makes 4-6 servings

Ingredients:

1 large egg
3/4 cup whole milk
1 white bread slice, torn into small pieces
1/2 pound ground beef
1/2 pound ground pork
1 small yellow onion, minced
1 teaspoon kosher salt
3 tablespoons unsalted butter
1/3 cup all purpose flour
1 1/2 cups beef stock
Kosher salt and fresh pepper to taste
1/2 cup heavy cream

Method:

1. Beat the egg in a medium bowl.
2. Add the milk and bread pieces to the bowl; mix well.
3. Add the beef, pork, onions and 1 teaspoon salt; mix well then cover and refrigerate for 1 hour.
4. Using a small ice cream scoop, form mixture into small meatballs; set aside.
5. Set timer to 20 minutes and let pressure cooker preheat for 5 minutes with the lid off.
6. Add the butter to the pressure cooker.
7. When butter has melted, stir in the flour using a wooden spoon; stir for 1 minute.
8. Add the stock then season with salt and pepper; stir until smooth.
9. Place meatballs into the pressure cooker; secure lid.
10. Set steam vent to **SEAL** and reset timer to 15 minutes.
11. When cooking is complete, let pressure release naturally (about 10 minutes).
12. Gently stir in the cream until combined before serving.

CHICKEN CURRY IN A HURRY

Makes 4-6 servings

Ingredients:

tablespoons ghee or butter	1 tablespoon powdered chicken bouillon, such as Maggi
tablespoons curry powder	2 tablespoons cornstarch
teaspoon ground turmeric	1 cup unsweetened coconut milk
medium yellow onion, chopped	1 teaspoon fresh ginger, finely grated
tablespoons ginger, chopped	Zest and juice of 1 lime
tablespoon garlic, chopped	2 teaspoons honey
tablespoons Thai red curry paste	Kosher salt to taste
chicken thighs	Fresh cilantro, for garnishing
cups water	

Method:

1. Set timer to 20 minutes and let pressure cooker preheat for 5 minutes with the lid off.
2. Add the ghee or butter.
3. When ghee or butter has melted, add the curry powder and turmeric; stir until fragrant.
4. Add the onions, chopped ginger, garlic and curry paste; stir again until fragrant.
5. Add the chicken, water and bouillon; secure lid.
6. Set steam vent to **SEAL** and reset timer to 12 minutes.
7. When cooking is complete, let pressure release naturally (about 10 minutes).
8. Carefully remove lid then reset timer to 10 minutes.
9. Stir the cornstarch into the coconut milk then pour into the pressure cooker; stir until it boils and thickens.
10. Turn off the pressure cooker then stir in the grated ginger, lime zest, lime juice and honey.
11. Add salt if desired, garnish with cilantro and serve.

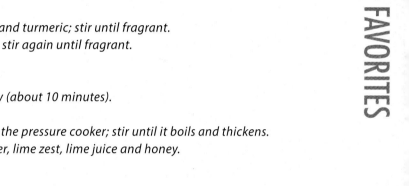

CHICKEN STEW
WITH DUMPLINGS

Makes 6 servings

For the Stew:

2 tablespoons unsalted butter
1 1/2 pounds chicken pieces
Kosher salt and fresh pepper to taste
2 tablespoons all purpose flour
1 teaspoon dried sage
3 carrots, cut into coins
2 celery stalks, sliced
1 large yellow onion, chopped
1 tablespoon powdered chicken bouillon, such as Maggi
2 1/2 cups water
1 cup whole milk

For the Dumplings:

2 cups all purpose flour
2 teaspoons baking powder
1 teaspoon kosher salt
1/2 cup unsalted butter, diced
3/4 cup buttermilk
2 tablespoons fresh parsley, chopped
1 cup frozen peas

FAVORITES

30

Method:

1. Set timer to 20 minutes and let pressure cooker preheat for 5 minutes with the lid off.
2. Add the butter to the pressure cooker.
3. Season chicken pieces with salt and pepper then sprinkle all over with flour.
4. When butter sizzles, add the chicken pieces and lightly brown on all sides.
5. Add remaining stew ingredients to the pressure cooker; stir then secure lid.
6. Set steam vent to **SEAL** and reset timer to 20 minutes.
7. While stew cooks, make the dumplings by placing the flour, baking powder, salt and butter into a mixing bowl; use a fork to combine and stir until crumbly.
8. Stir the buttermilk and parsley into the dumpling mixture; set aside.
9. When cooking is complete, let pressure release naturally (about 10 minutes).
10. Carefully remove lid then reset timer to 7 minutes.
11. Add the peas then drop dumpling batter by the tablespoons into the bubbling stew.
12. Place lid onto the pressure cooker but do not lock it to avoid cooking under pressure.
13. Let cook for 7 minutes or until dumplings are done.
14. Serve hot.

TIP

For a different type of dumpling you can substitute corn meal for the flour. If you are allergic to gluten, you can easily make these dumplings using gluten-free flour mix.

TASTES LIKE PIZZA CASSEROLE

Makes 4-6 servings

Ingredients:

2 tablespoons olive oil
1 pound Italian sausage, crumbled
1 large yellow onion, chopped
6 garlic cloves, minced
1 green bell pepper, diced
1 teaspoon Italian seasoning
1 package (4 ounces) sliced pepperoni
3 cups dry ring-shaped pasta
2 cups chicken stock
2 cups tomato sauce
Kosher salt and fresh pepper to taste
1 cup mozzarella cheese, shredded
1/2 cup Parmesan cheese, shredded
Crusty Italian bread, for serving

Method:

1. Set timer to 20 minutes and let pressure cooker preheat for 5 minutes with the lid off.
2. Add the oil to the pressure cooker.
3. When oil is hot, add the crumbled sausage, onions and garlic; stir until sausage is cooked through (drain off some of the fat if desired).
4. Add remaining ingredients, except cheeses and bread; stir then secure lid.
5. Set steam vent to **SEAL** and reset timer to 6 minutes.
6. When cooking is complete, carefully release the pressure manually (see tips on page 7) then remove lid.
7. Add the cheeses then replace lid without locking it and let cheese melt for a few minutes.
8. Garnish as desired and serve with bread.

WOLF'S REISFLEISCH

Makes 6 servings

Ingredients:

4 tablespoons unsalted butter
1 cup bell peppers, diced
1 cup yellow onions, diced
1/2 cup celery, diced
1/2 cup carrots, diced
1 garlic clove, minced
2 cups long-grain rice, uncooked
2 cups chicken stock
2 teaspoons fresh lemon juice
1 tablespoon paprika
Kosher salt and fresh pepper to taste
Chili flakes to taste
1 pound smoked sausage, sliced into chunks
2 tablespoons fresh parsley, for garnishing

Method:

1. Set timer to 20 minutes and let pressure cooker preheat for 5 minutes with the lid off.
2. Add the butter to the pressure cooker.
3. When butter sizzles, add the bell peppers, onions, celery, carrots and garlic; sauté until vegetables are well browned.
4. Add remaining ingredients, except parsley; stir well then secure lid.
5. Set steam vent to **SEAL** and timer to 6 minutes.
6. When cooking is complete, let pressure release naturally (about 10 minutes).
7. Fluff the rice, garnish with parsley and serve hot.

GOOEY CHOCOLATE MALTED CAKE

Makes 4-6 servings

Ingredients:
1 1/2 cups all purpose flour
3/4 cup granulated sugar
3 tablespoons malted milk powder
3 tablespoons cocoa powder
1 teaspoon baking soda
1/2 teaspoon kosher salt
1 teaspoon pure vanilla extract
1/4 cup vegetable oil
1 cup water
1 tablespoon white vinegar
1 1/2 cups water
1 cup crushed malted milk balls

Method:
1. Place all ingredients, except water and malted milk balls, in the order listed above into a mixing bowl; whisk using a hand whisk until smooth (batter will be runny).
2. Apply nonstick spray to a round cake pan that fits inside the pressure cooker.
3. Pour batter into the pan then cover with aluminum foil.
4. Place a metal rack into the bottom of the pressure cooker.
5. Make a foil sling for the cake pan (see page 8).
6. Pour the water into the pressure cooker then lower the cake pan into the pressure cooker using the foil sling; secure lid.
7. Set steam vent to **VENT** (not **SEAL** as you will not be cooking under pressure).
8. Set timer to 30 minutes and a separate kitchen timer to 30 minutes (setting the pressure cooker timer to 30 minutes will turn the cooker on but the timer will not count down because you are not cooking under pressure).
9. After 30 minutes of cooking, remove lid then check for doneness by inserting a wooden pick off-center, it should only have a few moist crumbs clinging to it.
10. Remove the cake pan by the foil sling and let cool until warm.
11. Top with crushed malted milk balls before serving.

TIP
This cake can easily be made gluten-free by substituting gluten-free baking mix for the all purpose flour.

CRÈME BRÛLÉE

Makes 4 servings

Ingredients:

1 3/4 cups heavy cream
1 vanilla bean, split (see source on page 106)
1/3 cup granulated sugar
6 large egg yolks
1 1/2 cups water
Additional granulated sugar for caramelizing tops

Method:

1. In a sauce pan over medium heat, combine the cream and vanilla bean.
2. Bring to a simmer (bubbles should form around the edges of the pan) then remove from heat.
3. Let cream mixture stand for 10 minutes to infuse the flavor from the vanilla bean.
4. In a bowl, whisk together the sugar and egg yolks until smooth.
5. Strain cream mixture into the sugar mixture then whisk to combine.
6. Divide mixture between 4 ramekins, filling them almost to the top then cover each with aluminum foil.
7. Place a metal rack into the bottom of the pressure cooker then add the water.
8. Place the ramekins into the pressure cooker; secure lid.
9. Set steam vent to **SEAL** and timer to 6 minutes.
10. When cooking is complete, let pressure release naturally (about 10 minutes).
11. Remove ramekins and chill for a minimum of 1 hour.
12. To serve, place the ramekins on a cookie sheet and remove the aluminum foil.
13. Sprinkle the top of each dessert with an even layer of sugar then use a blow torch (see source page 106) to caramelize the sugar.
14. Let rest for 5 minutes to allow the sugar to cool before serving.

TIP

If you do not have a blow torch you can make the Microwave Caramel (see page 105) and pour a layer of this caramel over the top of each Crème Brûlée for a similar effect.

CHOCOLATE TRUFFLE CRÈME BRÛLÉE

Makes 6 servings

Ingredients:

- cups heavy whipping cream
- cup bittersweet chocolate pieces or chips
- /3 cup granulated sugar
- teaspoons vanilla extract
- large egg yolks
- 1/2 cups water
- dditional granulated sugar for caramelizing tops

Method:

1. Heat the whipping cream in the microwave for 2 minutes or until very hot.
2. Place the chocolate pieces into a large bowl then add the hot cream; whisk until chocolate is completely melted.
3. Whisk in the sugar, vanilla and egg yolks.
4. Divide the mixture between 6 ramekins then cover each ramekin with aluminum foil.
5. Place a metal rack into the bottom of the pressure cooker.
6. Pour the water into the pressure cooker then place ramekins inside the pressure cooker (stack them in a pyramid fashion or cook in 2 batches); secure lid.
7. Set steam vent to **SEAL** and timer to 6 minutes.
8. When cooking is complete, let pressure release naturally (about 10 minutes).
9. Remove ramekins and chill for a minimum of 1 hour.
10. To serve, place the ramekins on a cookie sheet and remove the aluminum foil.
11. Sprinkle the top of each dessert with an even layer of sugar then use a blow torch (see source page 106) to caramelize the sugar (if you do not have a blow torch you can make the Microwave Caramel on page 105 and pour a layer of caramel over the top of each dessert).
12. Let rest for 5 minutes to allow the sugar to cool before serving.

VANILLA BEAN CHEESECAKE

Makes 6-8 servings

Ingredients:
1 cup graham cracker crumbs
2 tablespoons unsalted butter
1 vanilla bean, split and scraped
16 ounces cream cheese, softened
3/4 cup granulated sugar
3 large eggs
1 teaspoon vanilla extract
1 1/2 cups water

Method:
1. To make the crust, mix together the graham crackers and butter in a bowl then press mixture into the bottom of 7-inch springform pan.
2. In a stand mixer, combine the vanilla bean seeds, cream cheese, sugar, eggs and vanilla extract; mix until sugar is dissolved.
3. Pour mixture over the crust in the springform pan then tightly cover with aluminum foil.
4. Place a metal rack into the bottom of the pressure cooker.
5. Make a foil sling for the springform pan (see page 8).
6. Pour the water into the pressure cooker then lower the springform pan into the pressure cooker using the foil sling; secure lid.
7. Set steam vent to **SEAL** and timer to 25 minutes.
8. When cooking is complete, let pressure release naturally (about 10 minutes).
9. Remove lid and let cool for 1 hour before removing the pan by the foil sling.
10. Chill in the refrigerator for a minimum of 8 hours before serving.

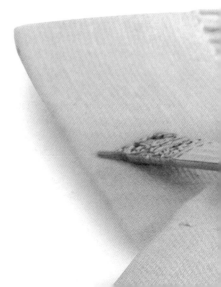

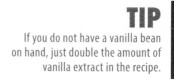

TIP

If you do not have a vanilla bean on hand, just double the amount of vanilla extract in the recipe.

FAVORITES

39

BACON & BROCCOLI
FRITTATA

Makes 4 servings

Ingredients:

8 bacon strips, diced
1 small yellow onion, diced
2 Russet potatoes, boiled and sliced
2 cups fresh broccoli florets
1/2 cup sun dried tomatoes in oil, drained
10 large eggs, beaten well
Kosher salt and fresh pepper to taste
1/2 cup Provolone cheese, shredded

Method:

1. Set timer to 20 minutes and let pressure cooker preheat for 5 minutes with the lid off.
2. Add the bacon; sauté bacon until soften then add the onions and sauté onions until browned.
3. Add remaining ingredients, except cheese; use a silicone spatula to push the eggs towards the center of the pressure cooker and allow the liquid part to flow underneath the cooked part.
4. When most of the eggs have set, top with cheese then secure lid.
5. Set steam vent to **VENT** (not **SEAL** as you will not be cooking under pressure).
6. Set timer to 5 minutes and a separate kitchen timer to 5 minutes (setting the pressure cooker timer to 5 minutes will turn the cooker on but the timer will not count down because you are not cooking under pressure).
7. Let cook for 3-5 minutes or until cheese has melted and eggs are set.
8. Use potholders and a silicone spatula to slide the frittata from the pressure cooker onto a serving plate.
9. Garnish as desired and serve hot, warm or cold.

BANANA FRENCH TOAST
BREAKFAST BAKE

Makes 4-6 servings

For the French Toast:

4 tablespoons unsalted butter
3/4 cup light brown sugar, packed
3 overripe bananas, pureed
1 tablespoon vanilla extract
1/2 teaspoon ground cinnamon
2 teaspoons fresh lemon juice
1/4 teaspoon kosher salt
3 cups half & half
6 large eggs
4 cups challah bread, cut into 2-inch cubes
1/2 cup pecan pieces, toasted
1 1/2 cups water

For Serving:

Butter
Banana slices
Syrup
Whipped cream

Method:

1. Melt the butter in a sauté pan over medium-high heat.
2. Add the sugar to the pan and stir until bubbly.
3. Stir in the banana puree, vanilla, cinnamon, lemon juice and salt; remove from heat.
4. In a bowl, whisk together the half & half and eggs then stir in the banana puree mixture.
5. Butter a 7-inch casserole dish that fits inside the pressure cooker.
6. Place the bread cubes and pecans into the casserole dish then pour the banana mixture over the bread.
7. Cover dish with aluminum foil then place a metal rack into the bottom of the pressure cooker.
8. Make a foil sling for the casserole dish (see page 8).
9. Pour the water into the pressure cooker then lower the casserole dish into the pressure cooker using the foil sling; secure lid.
10. Set steam vent to **SEAL** and timer to 25 minutes.
11. When cooking is complete, let pressure release naturally (about 10 minutes).
12. Remove lid then remove the casserole dish by the foil sling.
13. Serve hot with butter, banana slices, syrup and whipped cream.

BREAKFAST SAUSAGE & CHEESE
CASSEROLE

Makes 4-6 servings

Ingredients:

1 tablespoon unsalted butter, softened
6 large eggs
3 cups half & half
1 teaspoon apple cider vinegar
1/4 cup fresh parsley, chopped
Kosher salt and fresh pepper to taste
2 cups bread (such as brioche), cut into 1-inch cubes
2 cups Russet potatoes, peeled and diced
1 small yellow onion, diced
1 green bell pepper, diced
1 pound breakfast sausage, crumbled
1 cup sharp Cheddar cheese, shredded
1/4 cup Parmesan cheese, grated
1 1/2 cups water

Method:

1. Butter a casserole dish that fits inside the pressure cooker then set aside.
2. In a bowl, use a hand whisk to combine the eggs, half & half, vinegar, parsley, salt and pepper; whisk until smooth.
3. Layer the bread cubes, potatoes, onions, bell peppers, sausage and cheeses into the prepared casserole dish.
4. Pour the egg mixture over the ingredients in the casserole dish then cover with aluminum foil.
5. Place a metal rack into the bottom of the pressure cooker.
6. Make a foil sling for the casserole dish (see page 8).
7. Pour the water into the pressure cooker then lower the casserole dish into the pressure cooker using the foil sling; secure lid.
8. Set steam vent to **SEAL** and timer to 25 minutes.
9. When cooking is complete, let pressure release naturally (about 10 minutes).
10. Remove, garnish as desired and serve hot.

STEEL CUT OATS
WITH BERRIES

Makes 3-4 servings

For the Oats:

1 cup steel cut oats
3 1/2 cups water
1/4 teaspoon kosher salt
2 teaspoons unsalted butter

For Serving:

Brown sugar
Mixed berries
Whole milk

Method:

1. Place all oats ingredients into the pressure cooker; secure lid.
2. Set steam vent to **SEAL** and timer to 5 minutes.
3. When cooking is complete, let pressure release naturally (about 10 minutes).
4. Spoon into serving bowls then serve with brown sugar, berries and milk.

WHOLE CHICKEN
SOUP

Makes 6 servings

Ingredients:

1 whole chicken (3-4 pounds)
1 medium onion, quartered
3 fresh dill sprigs
3 fresh thyme sprigs
2 carrots, cut on the bias
1 celery stalk, cut on the bias
1 large leek, white and light green part only, sliced
6 cups chicken stock
8 whole peppercorns
1 1/2 teaspoons kosher salt, or to taste

Method:

1. *Place all ingredients into the pressure cooker; secure lid.*
2. *Set steam vent to **SEAL** and timer to 35 minutes.*
3. *When cooking is complete, let pressure release naturally (about 10 minutes).*
4. *Use tongs to pull chicken apart then garnish as desired and serve.*

SPLIT PEA & BACON SOUP

akes 4-6 servings

ngredients:

tablespoons unsalted butter
garlic cloves, minced
medium yellow onion, peeled and diced
pound dried split peas
bacon strips, cooked and crumbled
cups chicken stock
bay leaf
osher salt and fresh pepper to taste

Method:

1. *Place all ingredients into the pressure cooker; secure lid.*
2. *Set steam vent to **SEAL** and timer to 10 minutes.*
3. *When cooking is complete, let pressure release naturally (about 10 minutes).*
4. *Taste and adjust seasoning if desired before serving.*

TIP

If you want a smoother consistency, you can puree the soup in batches using a blender or immersion blender until desired consistency.

BUTTERNUT SQUASH SOUP

Makes 4 servings

Ingredients:

6 cups butternut squash, cut into 1-inch cubes
2 tablespoons powdered chicken bouillon, such as Maggi
2 teaspoons kosher salt
1/2 teaspoon fresh pepper
1/2 teaspoon ground cinnamon
Water, as needed
2 teaspoons fresh chives, chopped
2 tablespoons honey

Method:

1. Place all ingredients, except water, chives and honey, into the pressure cooker.
2. Add enough water to the pressure cooker until the squash is almost covered; secure lid.
3. Set steam vent to **SEAL** and timer to 6 minutes.
4. When cooking is complete, let pressure release naturally (about 10 minutes).
5. Use an immersion blender to puree the soup until desired consistency is achieved.
6. Adjust seasoning if desired then garnish with chives and honey before serving.

TIP

If you don't have an immersion blender, you can puree the soup in small batches using a blender. For a chunkier consistency, you can also use a potato masher.

BEEF & BARLEY STEW

Makes 4 servings

Ingredients:

1/4 pounds lean ground beef
can (28 ounces) crushed tomatoes
1/3 cups water
/2 cup barley
large carrots, peeled and cut into 1/4-inch coins
celery stalks, cut into 1/4-inch slices
large Russet potato, peeled and diced
medium white onion, peeled and diced
garlic clove, peeled and minced
/2 teaspoon dried thyme
/2 teaspoon dried rosemary
/2 teaspoon dried marjoram
osher salt and fresh pepper to taste

Method:

1. Set timer to 20 minutes and let pressure cooker preheat for 5 minutes with the lid off.
2. Add the ground beef; stir and cook until browned then drain excess fat.
3. Place remaining ingredients into the pressure cooker; stir then secure lid.
4. Set steam vent to **SEAL** and reset timer to 20 minutes.
5. When cooking is complete, let pressure release naturally (about 10 minutes).
6. Taste and adjust seasoning if desired and serve.

BBQ BEANS

Makes 4-6 servings

Ingredients:

1 pound dried navy beans, soaked for 4 hours
1 tablespoon canola oil
1/2 small yellow onion, diced
1 tablespoon store-bought ketchup
2 tablespoons bottled BBQ sauce
1/4 cup honey
1/2 cup brown sugar
1 1/3 cups water
Kosher salt to taste

Method:

1. *Place all ingredients into the pressure cooker; stir then secure lid.*
2. *Set steam vent to **SEAL** and timer to 15 minutes.*
3. *When cooking is complete, let pressure release naturally (about 10 minutes).*
4. *Taste and adjust seasoning if desired and serve.*

BEGINNINGS & SIDES

QUICK COOKED
COLLARD GREENS

Makes 6 servings

For the Collard Greens:

1 smoked ham hock or 8 ounces ham chunks
Kosher salt and fresh pepper to taste
4 cups chicken stock
1 teaspoon chili flakes (optional)
2 bunches fresh collard greens, washed and chopped

For Serving:

Bottled Pepper sauce, such as Texas Pete
Cornbread

Method:

1. Place the ham, salt, pepper, stock and chili flakes if desired into the pressure cooker; keep lid off.
2. Set timer to 8 minutes.
3. When stock begins to boil, add some collard greens then add more as they cook down.
4. When all the collard greens have been added, secure lid and set steam vent to **SEAL** (leave timer at 8 minutes).
5. When cooking is complete, let pressure release naturally (about 10 minutes).
6. Taste and adjust seasoning if desired then serve with pepper sauce and cornbread.

MEXICAN RICE

Makes 3 cups

Ingredients:

2 bacon strips, cut into small pieces
1 small yellow onion, diced
1 cup long-grain white rice, uncooked
1 3/4 cups chicken stock
3/4 cup prepared salsa
1/4 cup tiny frozen peas, thawed
1/4 cup fresh cilantro, minced
Kosher salt to taste

Method:

1. *Set timer to 20 minutes and let pressure cooker preheat for 5 minutes with the lid off.*
2. *Add the bacon and onions to the pressure cooker; cook until most of the fat has rendered off the bacon.*
3. *Add the rice and cook for 1 minute.*
4. *Add the stock and salsa; secure lid.*
5. *Set steam vent to **SEAL** and reset timer to 7 minutes.*
6. *When cooking is complete, let pressure release naturally (about 10 minutes).*
7. *Stir in remaining ingredients and adjust seasoning if desired.*
8. *Garnish as desired and serve.*

BRUSSELS SPROUTS

Makes 4 servings

Ingredients:

bacon strips, diced
medium yellow onion, diced
pound Brussels sprouts, ends trimmed and cut in half
1/2 cup chicken stock
teaspoon granulated sugar
teaspoon vinegar
kosher salt and fresh pepper to taste

Method:

1. Set timer to 20 minutes and let pressure cooker preheat for 5 minutes with the lid off.
2. Add the bacon and onions; cook for 5 minutes or until onions are translucent.
3. Place remaining ingredients into the pressure cooker; secure lid.
4. Set steam vent to **SEAL** and reset timer to 2 minutes.
5. When cooking is complete, let pressure release naturally (about 10 minutes).
6. Serve immediately.

TIP
You can turn this into a vegetarian dish by removing the bacon and substituting the chicken stock with water.

BROCCOLI & RICE
CASSEROLE

Makes 3 1/2 cups

Ingredients:

2 tablespoons unsalted butter
1 small yellow onion, minced
1 cup long-grain white rice, uncooked
1 1/4 cup chicken stock
1 cup whole milk
1 large stalk broccoli, cut into small florets
4 ounces Monterey Jack cheese, shredded
1/4 cup fresh parsley, finely chopped
Kosher salt and fresh pepper to taste

Method:

1. Set timer to 20 minutes and let pressure cooker preheat for 5 minutes with the lid off.
2. Add the butter to the pressure cooker.
3. When butter sizzles, add the onions and cook until soft.
4. Add the rice and cook for 1 minute.
5. Add the stock and milk; secure lid.
6. Set steam vent to **SEAL** and reset timer to 7 minutes.
7. When cooking is complete, let pressure release naturally (about 10 minutes).
8. Remove lid then gently stir in the broccoli; reset timer to 3 minutes and cook uncovered.
9. Stir in remaining ingredients, adjust seasoning if desired and serve.

CAULIFLOWER WITH
CHEESE SAUCE

Makes 3-4 servings

Ingredients:

1/3 cups evaporated milk
1 tablespoon unsalted butter, melted
1/2 small yellow onion, diced
1 tablespoon powdered chicken bouillon, such as Maggi
1/2 cup American cheese, shredded
1/3 cup Cheddar cheese, shredded
1/3 cup mozzarella cheese, shredded
1 cauliflower head, cut into small pieces
Kosher salt and fresh pepper to taste

Method:

1. Place all ingredients, except cauliflower, salt and pepper, into the pressure cooker; stir to combine.
2. Add the cauliflower, salt and pepper then stir gently to coat; secure lid.
3. Set steam vent to **SEAL** and timer to 2 minutes.
4. When cooking is complete, carefully release the pressure manually (see tips on page 7) then remove lid.
5. Taste and adjust seasoning if desired before serving.

ARTICHOKES WITH
LEMON VINAIGRETTE

Makes 4 servings

For the Artichokes:

4 medium artichokes, trimmed
1 1/2 cups water
1 teaspoon kosher salt
1 lemon, sliced, divided

For the Lemon Vinaigrette:

1/2 cup olive oil
3 tablespoons fresh lemon juice
1 tablespoon white onions, finely chopped
1 1/2 teaspoons Dijon mustard
1/2 teaspoon lemon peel, grated
1/2 teaspoon granulated sugar
Kosher salt and fresh pepper to taste

Method:

1. Place the artichokes, water, salt and half of the lemon slices into the pressure cooker; secure lid.
2. Set steam vent to **SEAL** and timer to 15 minutes.
3. In a bowl, combine all vinaigrette ingredients; mix well then set aside.
4. When cooking is complete, let pressure release naturally (about 10 minutes).
5. Remove artichokes using tongs, garnish with remaining lemon slices and serve with vinaigrette.

TIP

If all you can find at the market are small baby artichokes, cook them for only half as long. Save the liquid after making these artichokes to use as a flavor boost in soups or stews.

SWEET SWEET POTATOES
WITH PECANS

Makes 4-6 servings

Ingredients:

3 sweet potatoes, peeled and cubed
2 tablespoons cornstarch
1 cup water
1/4 cup brown sugar
1/4 cup granulated sugar
1/4 cup honey
2 tablespoons unsalted butter
1/2 cup pecans, chopped

Method:

1. In a bowl, toss the sweet potatoes in cornstarch until evenly coated.
2. Transfer sweet potatoes to the pressure cooker.
3. Add remaining ingredients, except pecans, to the pressure cooker; secure lid.
4. Set steam vent to **SEAL** and timer to 4 minutes.
5. When cooking is complete, carefully release the pressure manually (see tips on page 7) then remove lid.
6. Stir in the pecans and serve.

SWEET POTATO PUREE WITH
GINGERSNAP COOKIES

Makes 4 servings

Ingredients:

pounds sweet potatoes, peeled and cubed
cup chicken stock
tablespoons unsalted butter
gingersnap cookies
osher salt and freshly cracked pepper to taste
cup half & half, divided

Method:

1. Place the potatoes and stock into the pressure cooker; secure lid.
2. Set steam vent to **SEAL** and timer to 8 minutes.
3. When cooking is complete, carefully release the pressure manually (see tips on page 7) then remove lid.
4. Remove and drain the potatoes.
5. Transfer drained potatoes to a food processor fitted with a metal "S" blade.
6. Add the butter, cookies, salt and pepper to the food processor.
7. Turn on the food processor; while processing, pour some half & half through the feed tube.
8. Stop the food processor, scrape down the mixture then add more half & half until smooth and velvety or until desired consistency is achieved.
9. Taste and adjust seasoning before serving.

SCALLOPED POTATOES
WITH HAM

Makes 4-6 servings

Ingredients:

10 small red potatoes, thinly sliced
1 tablespoon powdered chicken bouillon, such as Maggi
1 1/3 cups evaporated milk
1/2 cup cooked ham, diced
1/2 cup Cheddar cheese, shredded
6 slices American cheese, diced
Kosher salt and fresh pepper to taste

Method:

1. *Place all ingredients into the pressure cooker; stir gently to combine then secure lid.*
2. *Set steam vent to **SEAL** and timer to 6 minutes.*
3. *When cooking is complete, carefully release the pressure manually (see tips on page 7) then remove lid.*
4. *Taste and adjust seasoning if desired and serve.*

SOUTHERN

POTATO SALAD

Makes 4-6 servings

Ingredients:

- pounds red potatoes, cut into 1/2-inch cubes
- cup chicken stock
- tablespoon apple cider vinegar
- 1/2 small yellow onion, diced
- celery stalk, diced
- tablespoons sweet pickle relish
- 1/2 cup mayonnaise
- tablespoons yellow mustard
- large eggs, hard boiled, chopped (optional)
- Kosher salt and fresh pepper to taste
- tablespoon fresh chives, finely chopped

Method:

1. Place the potatoes, stock and vinegar into the pressure cooker; secure lid.
2. Set steam vent to **SEAL** and timer to 6 minutes.
3. While potatoes are cooking, combine remaining ingredients, except chives, in a bowl.
4. When cooking is complete, carefully release the pressure manually (see tips on page 7) then remove lid.
5. Transfer potatoes to the bowl then carefully stir to combine, making sure not to mash the potatoes.
6. Garnish with chives before serving.

COMPANY HASSELBACK
POTATOES

Makes 4-6 servings

Ingredients:

6 medium Yukon potatoes, peeled
4 tablespoons unsalted butter
1 large white onion, thinly sliced
2 garlic cloves, chopped
2 teaspoons fresh thyme leaves
Kosher salt and fresh pepper to taste
1 cup chicken stock
1 tablespoon fresh parsley, chopped

Method:

1. *Place a potato vertically on a cutting board in front of you.*
2. *Insert 2 chopsticks or wooden spoon handles lengthwise on either side of the potato.*
3. *Cut slices down the potato, 1/8-inch apart, until the knife hits the chopsticks or spoons to prevent the knife from cutting all the way through the potato; repeat with remaining potatoes.*
4. *Set timer to 20 minutes and let pressure cooker preheat for 5 minutes with the lid off.*
5. *Add the butter to the pressure cooker.*
6. *When butter has melted, add the onions and garlic; stir until slightly translucent.*
7. *Place the potatoes, cut-side up, into the pressure cooker then spoon some of the butter over them.*
8. *Sprinkle potatoes with thyme, salt and pepper then pour the stock into the pressure cooker; secure lid.*
9. *Set steam vent to **SEAL** and reset timer to 6 minutes.*
10. *When cooking is complete, carefully release the pressure manually (see tips on page 7) then remove lid.*
11. *Sprinkle with parsley and serve hot with some of the butter and onions.*

TIP

To make prettier potatoes, rinse the potatoes after slicing them. This removes some of the starch naturally present in the potatoes and allows the cuts to fan out more easily.

FASTEST
MASHED POTATOES

Makes 4 servings

Ingredients:

1 cup water
6 large Russet potatoes, peeled and cubed
4 tablespoons unsalted butter, melted and hot
1 cup hot whole milk or half & half (or more, depending on your desired texture)
Kosher salt and fresh pepper to taste

Method:

1. Pour the water into the pressure cooker then add the potatoes; secure lid.
2. Set steam vent to **SEAL** and timer to 6 minutes.
3. When cooking is complete, carefully release the pressure manually (see tips on page 7) then remove lid.
4. Drain potatoes then mash them using a potato masher or pass potatoes through a ricer or food mill.
5. Add the butter and some salt; stir until incorporated.
6. Add enough milk or half & half and mix until soft and creamy (do not over mix or texture will become gluey).
7. Taste and adjust seasoning with salt and pepper if desired before serving.

TIP

It is important to add the butter before adding the milk or half & half when mashing the potatoes because the fat from the butter coats all of the potato starch and helps prevent the "gluey" texture that can occur when mashing potatoes.

BOSTON
BROWN BREAD
Makes 2 mini loaves

Ingredients:
3/4 cup unbleached all purpose flour
1/2 cup 100% whole wheat flour
1/4 cup rye flour
1/2 cup yellow cornmeal
1 teaspoon ground cinnamon
1/2 teaspoon kosher salt
1/2 teaspoon baking soda
1 cup buttermilk
1/3 cup molasses
1/2 cup dark raisins
1 1/2 cups water

Method:
1. Apply nonstick spray to 2 mini loaf pans that will fit inside the pressure cooker.
2. In a large bowl, whisk together the flours, cornmeal, cinnamon, salt and baking soda using a hand whisk.
3. Whisk in the buttermilk, molasses and raisins.
4. Spoon batter evenly into the prepared pans until each is 3/4 full then cover pans tightly with aluminum foil.
5. Place a metal rack into the bottom of the pressure cooker then add the water.
6. Place pans into the pressure cooker (do not stack); secure lid.
7. Set steam vent to **VENT** (not **SEAL** as you will not be cooking under pressure).
8. Set timer to 45 minutes and a separate kitchen timer to 45 minutes (setting the pressure cooker timer to 45 minutes will turn the cooker on but the timer will not count down because you are not cooking under pressure).
9. After 45 minutes of cooking, remove lid then test for doneness by inserting a toothpick off-center; it should come out with just a few moist crumbs clinging to it.
10. Remove pans and let cool for 1 hour before serving.

SPAGHETTI
SQUASH

Makes 3-4 servings

Ingredients:

1 1/3 cups water
1 medium spaghetti squash, cut lengthwise
2 tablespoons unsalted butter
1 garlic clove, minced
1 teaspoon kosher salt
Tomato sauce and pesto, for serving

Method:

1. *Place a metal trivet into the bottom of the pressure cooker.*
2. *Pour the water into the pressure cooker.*
3. *Season squash with butter, garlic and salt.*
4. *Place squash, cut-side down, on top of the trivet inside the pressure cooker; secure lid.*
5. *Set steam vent to **SEAL** and timer to 15 minutes.*
6. *When cooking is complete, let pressure release naturally (about 10 minutes).*
7. *Carefully remove the squash then use a fork to rake out strands.*
8. *Garnish as desired and serve with tomato sauce and pesto.*

SCALLOPED CORN

Makes 4-6 servings

Ingredients:

1 1/2 cups water
1 1/2 cups fresh or frozen corn
2 green onions, sliced
2 large eggs, beaten
10 saltine cracker, crushed
1/3 cup Parmesan cheese, grated
1 cup half & half
2 teaspoons granulated sugar
2 teaspoons kosher salt
fresh pepper to taste

Method:

1. Apply nonstick cooking spray to 6 ramekins; set aside.
2. Place a metal rack into the bottom of the pressure cooker then add the water.
3. In a large bowl, combine remaining ingredients; mix well using a spoon.
4. Divide the mixture between the ramekins then cover each with aluminum foil.
5. Place ramekins into the pressure cooker (you may have to stack them like a pyramid); secure lid.
6. Set steam vent to **SEAL** and timer to 10 minutes.
7. When cooking is complete, let pressure release naturally (about 10 minutes).
8. Garnish as desired and serve hot or warm.

TIP

For a spicier version, fold in 1 chopped jalapeño, 1/4 cup diced red bell peppers and a small handful of chopped cilantro before spooning into the ramekins.

EASY PRESSURE
COOKER LASAGNA

Makes 4-6 servings

Ingredients:

1 1/2 cups beef stock
1 pound Italian sausage, crumbled and cooked
1 large yellow onion, chopped
4 garlic cloves, chopped
1 tablespoon Italian seasoning
Kosher salt and fresh pepper to taste
3 cups marinara sauce, divided
1 cup Parmesan cheese, grated
2 large eggs
2 cups ricotta cheese
3 cups broken lasagna noodles, uncooked
1 cup mozzarella cheese, shredded
2 tablespoons fresh parsley, chopped

Method:

1. Pour the stock into the pressure cooker.
2. Add the sausage, onions, garlic, Italian seasoning, salt and pepper; stir.
3. Pour half of the marinara sauce over the pressure cooker contents.
4. In a bowl, stir together the Parmesan, eggs and ricotta; dollop mixture over the pressure cooker contents.
5. Place noodles over the pressure cooker contents then pour remaining marinara sauce over the top; secure lid.
6. Set steam vent to **SEAL** and timer to 20 minutes.
7. When cooking is complete, let pressure release naturally (about 10 minutes).
8. Remove lid then top lasagna with mozzarella cheese and parsley; cover loosely with lid and let stand for 10 minutes or until cheese is melted.
9. Serve hot.

ENTREES

SAVORY BEEF
SHORT RIBS

Makes 4-6 servings

Ingredients:
- 2 tablespoons olive oil
- 8 meaty beef short ribs
- 2 tablespoons all purpose flour
- Kosher salt and fresh pepper to taste
- 1 large yellow onion, chopped
- 2 large carrots, peeled and chopped
- 1 Golden Delicious apple, peeled, cored and chopped
- 1/2 cup prunes, pitted
- 4 garlic cloves, minced
- 2 bay leaves
- 3 sprigs fresh thyme
- 1/2 cup store-bought ketchup
- 1 cup red wine
- 1 cup beef stock

Method:
1. Set timer to 20 minutes and let pressure cooker preheat for 5 minutes with the lid off.
2. Add the oil to the pressure cooker.
3. Dredge beef with flour then season with salt and pepper.
4. When oil is hot, add the beef in batches and brown both sides.
5. Place all of the beef and remaining ingredients into the pressure cooker; secure lid.
6. Set steam vent to **SEAL** and reset timer to 30 minutes.
7. When cooking is complete, let pressure release naturally (about 10 minutes).
8. Garnish as desired and serve hot.

JULIA'S BOEUF BOURGUIGNON

Makes 4-6 servings

For the Boeuf Bourguignon:

1 tablespoon olive oil
6 ounces bacon, julienned
3 pounds rump roast, cut into 2-inch cubes
1 carrot, sliced
1 large white onion, sliced
2 tablespoons all purpose flour
1 teaspoon kosher salt
1/4 teaspoon fresh pepper
1 cup full bodied red wine
1 cup beef stock
1 tablespoon tomato paste
2 garlic cloves, mashed
1 bay leaf, crumbled
18 pearl onions, peeled
1 pound button mushrooms, quartered

For Serving:

Fresh parsley
Potatoes, noodles or rice, cooked

Method:

1. Set timer to 20 minutes and let pressure cooker preheat for 5 minutes with the lid off.
2. Add the oil to the pressure cooker.
3. When oil is hot, add the bacon and sauté until lightly browned; remove and set aside.
4. Pat the roast cubes dry then sauté in batches in the pressure cooker until browned; remove and set aside.
5. Sauté the carrots and onions in the pressure cooker until browned; remove and set aside.
6. Discard excess fat from the pressure cooker then return the roast cubes and bacon to the pressure cooker; sprinkle with flour, salt and pepper then toss to coat.
7. Stir in the carrots, onions and remaining boeuf bourguignon ingredients; secure lid.
8. Set steam vent to **SEAL** and reset timer to 22 minutes.
9. When cooking is complete, let pressure release naturally (about 10 minutes).
10. Skim excess fat from the surface then adjust seasoning if desired.
11. Garnish with parsley and serve hot over potatoes, noodles or rice.

DAD'S TURN TO COOK PASTA

Makes 4-5 servings

Ingredients:

1 pound ground beef, crumbled

3 cups dry elbow macaroni, or other small pasta

2 1/2 cups beef stock or water

3 cups pasta sauce

1 package (1 ounce) ranch dressing mix

1 cup green peas, thawed (optional)

1 cup mozzarella cheese, shredded

Method:

1. *Place all ingredients, except peas and cheese, into the pressure cooker; stir then secure lid.*
2. *Set steam vent to **SEAL** and timer to 20 minutes.*
3. *When cooking is complete, let pressure release naturally (about 10 minutes).*
4. *Add the peas if desired then top with mozzarella cheese before serving.*

ENTREES

FRENCH DIP

SANDWICHES

Makes 4-6 servings

Ingredients:

2 pounds boneless beef chuck roast
1 large yellow onion, sliced
1 teaspoon dried thyme
3 cups beef stock
1 bay leaf
2 garlic cloves, minced
4-6 Provolone cheese slices
4-6 hoagie rolls

Method:

1. Place all ingredients, except cheese and hoagie rolls, into the pressure cooker; secure lid.
2. Set steam vent to **SEAL** and timer to 45 minutes.
3. When cooking is complete, let pressure release naturally (about 10 minutes).
4. Remove the roast from the pressure cooker then shred it using tongs or forks.
5. Place cheese on rolls then top with beef roast.
6. Ladle cooking juice from the pressure cooker into small dishes for dipping and serve.

SHREDDED FLANK STEAK

Makes 4-6 servings

For the Steak:

- pounds flank steak
- garlic cloves, chopped
- large yellow onion, sliced
- red bell pepper, diced
- tablespoon dried oregano
- teaspoon dried thyme
- teaspoon cumin seed
- /2 cup tomato paste
- tablespoon red wine vinegar
- tablespoon powdered beef bouillon, such as Maggi
- cups water
- Kosher salt and fresh pepper to taste

For Serving:

Fresh cilantro, chopped
White onions, chopped

Method:

1. Place all steak ingredients into the pressure cooker; stir well to dissolve the tomato paste then secure lid.
2. Set steam vent to **SEAL** and timer to 45 minutes.
3. When cooking is complete, let pressure release naturally (about 10 minutes).
4. Remove the meat, shred using tongs then return to the pressure cooker and stir.
5. Taste and adjust seasoning if desired then serve hot with chopped cilantro and onions.

ONE POT BEEF
BOLOGNESE

Makes 6 servings

Ingredients:

1 tablespoon unsalted butter
1 small yellow onion, chopped
1 carrot, chopped
1 celery stalk, chopped
2 garlic cloves, chopped
1 pound lean ground beef
3 tablespoons tomato paste
2 cups chicken stock
1 can (28 ounces) diced tomatoes
3 tablespoons heavy cream
3 cups pasta such as orecchiette, uncooked
Kosher salt and fresh pepper to taste

Method:

1. Set timer to 20 minutes and let pressure cooker preheat for 5 minutes with the lid off.
2. Add the butter to the pressure cooker.
3. When butter sizzles, add the onions, carrots, celery and garlic; sauté until browned.
4. Crumble in the beef then add remaining ingredients; stir well to dissolve the tomato paste then secure lid.
5. Set steam vent to **SEAL** and timer to 20 minutes.
6. When cooking is complete, let pressure release naturally (about 10 minutes).
7. Garnish as desired and serve hot.

SOUTHWEST CHILI CON CARNE

Makes 4-6 servings

Ingredients:

bacon slices, diced
pounds beef brisket, trimmed and cut into 1-inch cubes, divided
tablespoons Ancho chili powder
tablespoons new Mexican red chili powder
tablespoon ground cumin seeds
tablespoon Mexican oregano leaves
kosher salt and fresh pepper to taste
large white onion, diced
garlic cloves, minced
cups water
cups canned tomato puree
teaspoon honey
Juice of 1 lime
diced jalapeño pepper (optional)
1/2 cups dried dark red kidney bean

Method:

1. Set timer to 20 minutes and let pressure cooker preheat for 5 minutes with the lid off.
2. Add the bacon; cook until most of the fat has rendered out of it; remove and set aside.
3. Add half of the beef and brown lightly on all sides; remove then repeat with remaining beef.
4. Return all of the beef and bacon to the pressure cooker then add remaining ingredients; stir and secure lid.
5. Set steam vent to **SEAL** and reset timer to 22 minutes.
6. When cooking is complete, let pressure release naturally (about 10 minutes).
7. Adjust seasoning if desired before serving.

TIP

If you prefer a thicker chili, turn pressure cooker back on. Combine 3 tablespoons masa harina with 2/3 cup cold water then stir mixture into the bubbling chili. Cook and stir chili with the lid off until thickened.

CHICKEN & SAUSAGE
WITH PEPPERS

Makes 4-6 servings

Ingredients:

1 tablespoon olive oil
12 ounces Italian sausage links
6 boneless, skinless chicken thighs
1 medium yellow onion, diced
2 medium green bell peppers, cut into 3/4-inch thick strips
2 garlic cloves, minced
2 tablespoon red wine vinegar
1 can (16 ounces) diced tomatoes, drained
Crushed red pepper flakes, to taste
Kosher salt and fresh pepper to taste

Method:

1. Set timer to 20 minutes and let pressure cooker preheat for 5 minutes with the lid off.
2. Add the oil to the pressure cooker.
3. When oil is hot, add the sausage and chicken; cook until well browned on all sides.
4. Add remaining ingredients to the pressure cooker; stir to combine then secure lid.
5. Set steam vent to **SEAL** and reset timer to 25 minutes.
6. When cooking is complete, let pressure release naturally (about 10 minutes).
7. Taste and adjust seasoning if desired before serving.

ENTREES

74

SAUSAGE & SAUERKRAUT
DINNER

Makes 4 servings

Ingredients:

bag (1 pound) fresh sauerkraut
pounds kielbasa or other smoked sausages
bacon slices, diced
carrots, peeled then cut into coins
celery stalk, sliced
cups beer, chicken stock or water
red skinned potatoes, scrubbed and halved
tablespoon fresh parsley, chopped

Method:

1. Place all ingredients, except parsley, into the pressure cooker; secure lid.
2. Set steam vent to **SEAL** and timer to 3 minutes.
3. When cooking is complete, let pressure release naturally (about 10 minutes).
4. Garnish with parsley and serve hot.

EASY PORK ROAST
WITH APPLES

Makes 4-6 servings

Ingredients:

3 tablespoons unsalted butter
3 pounds pork shoulder or butt
Kosher salt and fresh pepper to taste
2 Granny Smith apples, sliced thickly
1 tablespoon chicken bouillon powder, such as Maggi
8 fresh sage leaves
1 medium yellow onion, thickly sliced
5 garlic cloves
1/3 cup light brown sugar, packed
2 cups apple juice
1 tablespoon apple cider vinegar

TIP

To thicken the cooking juices into gravy, remove the pork to a platter after it's done cooking, reset the pressure cooker to 20 minutes and leave the lid off. When juices are boiling, stir in 2 tablespoons of cornstarch that has been dissolved in 3 tablespoons of cold water. Stir until it boils again and has thickened then serve over the pork.

Method:

1. Set timer to 20 minutes and let pressure cooker preheat for 5 minutes with the lid off.
2. Add the butter to the pressure cooker.
3. When butter sizzles, add the pork then season with salt and pepper; brown pork for 5 minutes on each side or until well browned.
4. Add remaining ingredients to the pressure cooker; secure lid.
5. Set steam vent to **SEAL** and timer to 40 minutes.
6. When cooking is complete, let pressure release naturally (about 10 minutes).
7. Stir the liquid inside the pressure cooker then skim off excess fat; taste and adjust seasoning if desired.
8. Use tongs to pull pork apart then garnish as desired before serving.
9. You can refrigerate leftovers for up to 4 days or freeze for up to 3 months.

PULLED PORK WITH ROOT BEER BBQ SAUCE

Makes 4 servings

For the Pulled Pork:

2 1/2 pounds pork shoulder or butt
1 1/2 cups root beer
1 teaspoon root beer extract (optional)
1 cup bottled BBQ sauce
Kosher salt and fresh pepper to taste

For Serving:

Coleslaw
Soft buns

Method:

1. Place all pulled pork ingredients into the pressure cooker; stir then secure lid.
2. Set steam vent to **SEAL** and timer to 40 minutes.
3. When cooking is complete, let pressure release naturally (about 10 minutes).
4. Using tongs, pull the pork into shreds then stir into the sauce.
5. Serve on buns with coleslaw on top.

ASIAN PORK ROAST WITH HOISIN VEGETABLES

Makes 4-6 servings

Ingredients:

1 tablespoon canola oil
4 pounds pork loin, cubed
Kosher salt and fresh pepper to taste
2 large red onions, quartered
1 Acorn squash, seeded and wedged
1 package (8 ounces) whole button mushrooms
1/4 cup bottled Hoisin sauce
1 tablespoon dark sesame oil
1/4 cup soy sauce
1 1/4 cups chicken stock

Method:

1. Set timer to 20 minutes and let pressure cooker preheat for 5 minutes with the lid off.
2. Add the oil to the pressure cooker.
3. Pat pork dry using paper towels then season with salt and pepper.
4. When oil is hot, add the pork and brown on all sides then add remaining ingredients.
5. Stir to coat the pork and vegetables with the dark sauce; secure lid.
6. Set steam vent to **SEAL** and reset timer to 40 minutes.
7. When cooking is complete, let pressure release naturally (about 10 minutes).
8. Garnish as desired and serve.

STUFFED PORK CHOPS

Makes 4 servings

For the Stuffing:

1 small yellow onion, diced
1 celery stalk, diced
1/2 Granny Smith apple, diced
1 cup cornbread, crumbled
1 large egg, beaten
1/4 teaspoon dried sage
Kosher salt and fresh pepper to taste
3 tablespoons apple juice, or as needed

For the Pork Chops:

4 pork chops, 1-inch thick each
1 tablespoon canola oil
1 cup chicken stock

Method:

1. *In a bowl combine all stuffing ingredients, except apple juice.*
2. *Add enough apple juice to the bowl to moisten the crumbs.*
3. *Cut a pocket into each pork chop, going all the way to the bone.*
4. *Fill each pocket with stuffing, press to close then season both sides of the pork chops with salt and pepper.*
5. *Set timer to 20 minutes and let pressure cooker preheat for 5 minutes with the lid off.*
6. *Add the oil to the pressure cooker.*
7. *When oil is hot, add the pork chops in batches and brown on both sides; remove chops and set aside.*
8. *Pour the stock into the pressure cooker then place pork chops back into the pressure cooker; secure lid.*
9. *Set steam vent to **SEAL** and reset timer to 25 minutes.*
10. *When cooking is complete, let pressure release naturally (about 10 minutes).*
11. *Garnish as desired before serving.*

HAM & BEAN
DINNER

Makes 4-6 servings

Ingredients:

2 cups dried black eyed peas, rinsed
2 tablespoons canola oil
1 cup ham, cut into 1/2-inch cubes
1 small onion, chopped
2 garlic cloves, diced
Kosher salt and fresh pepper to taste
Water, as needed

Method:

1. Place all ingredients into the pressure cooker and add enough water to cover the beans; secure lid.
2. Set steam vent to **SEAL** and timer to 8 minutes.
3. When cooking is complete, let pressure release naturally (about 10 minutes).
4. Garnish as desired and serve immediately.

ENTREES

LAMB SHANKS WITH PORT WINE SAUCE

Makes 2 servings

Ingredients:

- 1 tablespoon olive oil
- 2 lamb shanks, 1 pound each
- Kosher salt and fresh pepper to taste
- 3 garlic cloves, peeled
- 1 cup beef stock
- 1/2 cup port wine
- 1 tablespoon tomato paste
- 1/2 teaspoon dried rosemary
- 1 tablespoon unsalted butter
- 2 teaspoons balsamic vinegar

Method:

1. Set timer to 20 minutes and let pressure cooker preheat for 5 minutes with the lid off.
2. Add the oil to the pressure cooker.
3. Season lamb shanks with salt and pepper.
4. When oil is hot, add the lamb shanks; cook until browned on all sides.
5. Add the garlic and cook until lightly browned.
6. Add remaining ingredients to the pressure cooker; stir and secure lid.
7. Set steam vent to **SEAL** and reset timer to 25 minutes.
8. When cooking is complete, let pressure release naturally (about 10 minutes).
9. Taste and adjust seasoning then garnish as desired before serving.

SALMON WITH SHIITAKE BROWN
RICE & EDAMAME

Makes 4 servings

For the Rice:

1 1/3 cup brown rice, uncooked
2 cups stock or water
1 bay leaf
2 tablespoons extra-virgin olive oil
1/2 cup dried shiitake mushrooms
1 tablespoon soy sauce
1 cup frozen edamame
2 garlic cloves, smashed
1/2 teaspoon sriracha or chili flakes
Kosher salt and fresh pepper to taste

For the Salmon:

4 salmon fillets
2 tablespoons soy sauce
1 tablespoon fresh ginger, julienned
2 green onions, julienned
2 garlic cloves, julienned

Method:

1. *Place all rice ingredients into the pressure cooker; stir and secure lid.*
2. *Set steam vent to **SEAL** and timer to 8 minutes.*
3. *While rice is cooking, arrange the salmon on a metal cake or pie pan that fits inside the pressure cooker.*
4. *Drizzle salmon with soy sauce then top with ginger, green onions and garlic; set aside.*
5. *When cooking is complete, carefully release the pressure manually (see tips on page 7) then remove lid.*
6. *Place the pan with the salmon on top of the rice inside the pressure cooker; secure lid.*
7. *Set steam vent to **SEAL** and timer to 2 minutes.*
8. *When cooking is complete, carefully release the pressure manually (see tips on page 7) then remove lid.*
9. *Garnish as desired before serving.*

TIP

If you don't like edamame, you can add a bag of frozen broccoli florets to the pressure cooker after cooking is complete and let stand for 5 minutes to thaw and heat the broccoli.

CAJUN SHRIMP
BOIL DINNER

Makes 6 servings

Ingredients:

1 large yellow onion, quartered
3 ears corn, cut in half
2 pounds small red bliss potatoes, halved
1 pound smoked sausage, cut into 2-inch slices
3 pounds shrimp, in the shells
1 lemon, halved
1 head garlic, cut in half lengthwise
3 tablespoons crab boil seasoning, such as Old Bay
1 bottle beer

Method:

1. Layer all ingredients into the pressure cooker in order listed; secure lid.
2. Set steam vent to **SEAL** and timer to 5 minutes.
3. When cooking is complete, let pressure release naturally (about 10 minutes).
4. Pour pressure cooker contents into a large colander to drain.
5. Serve hot.

TIP

This is a great recipe to try authentic Creole-style sausages. If you can only find Kielbasa or other smoked sausage, the dish will still taste great.

LINGUINE WITH CLAMS DINNER

Makes 4 servings

Ingredients:

2 tablespoons olive oil
4 garlic cloves, chopped
1 tablespoon fresh parsley, chopped
1 small yellow onion, chopped
1/2 teaspoon dried thyme
1/4 teaspoon chili flakes, or to taste
1/2 cup dry white wine
1/2 cup half & half
1 cup bottled clam juice
2 cups uncooked linguini pasta, broken into thirds
2 cups broccoli florets
1 pound small clams, cleaned

Method:

1. Set timer to 20 minutes and let pressure cooker preheat for 5 minutes with the lid off.
2. Add the oil to the pressure cooker.
3. When oil is hot, add the garlic, parsley and onions; sauté until fragrant and onions are translucent.
4. Add the thyme, chili flakes, wine, half & half, clam juice and pasta; stir well then secure lid.
5. Set steam vent to **SEAL** and reset timer to 6 minutes.
6. When cooking is complete, carefully release the pressure manually (see tips on page 7) then remove lid.
7. Stir in remaining ingredients; secure lid.
8. Set steam vent to **VENT** (not **SEAL** as you will not be cooking under pressure).
9. Set timer to 5 minutes and a separate kitchen timer to 5 minutes (setting the pressure cooker timer to 5 minutes will turn the cooker on but the timer will not count down because you are not cooking under pressure).
10. After 5 minutes of cooking, remove lid and stir (clams should all be open or cook for an additional 1-2 minutes if necessary).
11. Garnish as desired and serve immediately.

SHRIMP WITH
GRITS

Makes 3-4 servings

For the Grits:
1 1/2 cups stone ground grits
4 cups water
1 teaspoon kosher salt
4 tablespoons unsalted butter, divided

For the Shrimp:
1 tablespoon olive oil
1 1/2 pounds large shrimp, peeled and deveined
Kosher salt and fresh pepper to taste
1 garlic clove, minced
1/2 teaspoon chili flakes
1 bunch green onions, finely chopped

Method:
1. Place grits, water and salt into the pressure cooker; secure lid.
2. Set steam vent to **SEAL** and timer to 5 minutes.
3. When cooking is complete, let pressure release naturally (about 10 minutes).
4. Remove lid then add 2 tablespoons butter to the pressure cooker; cover.
5. Preheat the oil and remaining butter in a large sauté pan over medium-high heat.
6. Pat shrimp dry using paper towels then season with salt and pepper.
7. Place the shrimp into the pan and toss for 3 minutes or until heated through (do not overcook).
8. Remove the shrimp then add the garlic, chili flakes and green onions to the pan; stir for 1 minute or until vegetables are soft and fragrant.
9. Serve grits in bowls, topped with shrimp and garlic mixture.

PRESSURE COOKER
JAMBALAYA

Makes 6 servings

Ingredients:

5 bacon strips, diced
4 boneless, skinless chicken thighs, quartered
2 cups long-grain white rice, uncooked
1 large yellow onion, chopped
2 celery stalks, chopped
1 green bell pepper, chopped
5 garlic cloves, chopped
1 pound andouille sausage, diced
1 bay leaf
1 teaspoon dried thyme
2 teaspoons pimentón smoked paprika
1 teaspoon chili flakes, or to taste
1 can (14.5 ounces) diced tomatoes
1 2/3 cups chicken stock
Kosher salt and freshly cracked pepper to taste
1 bunch green onions, chopped

Method:

1. *Set timer to 20 minutes and let pressure cooker preheat for 5 minutes with the lid off.*
2. *Add the bacon to the pressure cooker; sauté until most of the fat has rendered out of the bacon then remove and set aside.*
3. *Add the chicken to the pressure cooker and brown lightly on all sides.*
4. *Add the rice and reserved bacon to the pressure cooker; stir to coat the rice with bacon fat.*
5. *Add remaining ingredients, except green onions, to the pressure cooker; stir well then secure lid.*
6. *Set steam vent to **SEAL** and reset timer to 6 minutes.*
7. *When cooking is complete, carefully release the pressure manually (see tips on page 7) then remove lid.*
8. *Fluff the rice, stir in the green onions and serve hot.*

TIP

If you prefer to use brown rice instead
of white rice in this recipe, add 5 more
minutes to the cooking time.

VEGGIE & PASTA
DINNER

Makes 4 servings

Ingredients:

3 tablespoons unsalted butter
1 large yellow onion, diced
1 small butternut squash, peeled and diced
4 cups dry rigatoni pasta
3 cups vegetable stock
1 celery stalk, diced
4 fresh sage leaves, torn
Kosher salt and fresh pepper to taste
3 ounces cream cheese, softened
1/4 cup Parmesan cheese, grated

Method:

1. Set timer to 20 minutes and let pressure cooker preheat for 5 minutes with the lid off.
2. Add the butter to the pressure cooker.
3. When butter sizzles, add the onions and stir.
4. Cook onions for 10 minutes or until very brown, stirring occasionally.
5. Add remaining ingredients, except cheeses; stir then secure lid.
6. Set steam vent to **SEAL** and timer to 6 minutes.
7. When cooking is complete, carefully release the pressure manually (see tips on page 7) then remove lid.
8. Stir in the cheeses until creamy.
9. Garnish as desired and serve hot.

GREEN
GUMBO

Makes 4-6 servings

Ingredients:

- 1 tablespoon apple cider vinegar
- 4 cups chicken stock
- 4 cups kielbasa sausage, cut into coins
- 1 tablespoon granulated sugar
- 1 teaspoon freshly ground pepper
- 1 teaspoon crushed red pepper flakes
- 1/2 cup canola oil
- 1/2 cup unbleached all purpose flour
- 2 pounds collard greens, divided

Method:

1. Place the vinegar, stock, sausage, sugar, pepper and chili flakes into the pressure cooker.
2. Set timer to 3 minutes and keep the lid off.
3. Preheat the oil in a saucepan over medium-high heat.
4. Add the flour to the saucepan and carefully whisk until it turns to a dark amber color.
5. Transfer the oil-flour mixture to the pressure cooker and stir immediately to prevent the oil-flour mixture from turning too dark.
6. Add 1 pound of collard greens to the pressure cooker and stir.
7. When collard greens wilted down, add remaining greens and stir again.
8. When greens have wilted to below the fill line of the pressure cooker, secure lid.
9. Set steam vent to **SEAL** and timer to 3 minutes.
10. When cooking is complete, let pressure release naturally (about 10 minutes).
11. Adjust seasoning and garnish as desired before serving.

ENTREES

TIP

Instead of collard greens, you can use kale, mustard greens or turnip greens.

PUMPKIN STUFFED WITH EVERYTHING GOOD

Makes 4 servings

Ingredients:

1 sugar or pie pumpkin, Kabocha or Acorn squash
Kosher salt and fresh pepper to taste
4 tablespoons unsalted butter
1 medium yellow onion, diced
4 garlic cloves, minced
2 cups Italian bread cubes
1 cup Swiss cheese, diced small

1/2 cup Parmesan cheese, grated
1 cup half & half or heavy cream
2 tablespoons fresh parsley, chopped
1 teaspoon fresh thyme
1 cup fresh spinach
A pinch of truffle salt (optional)
1 1/2 cups water

Method:

1. Cut the top off the pumpkin then scrape out all the seeds.
2. Sprinkle salt and pepper inside the pumpkin and on the underside of the pumpkin top.
3. In a skillet over medium-high heat, melt the butter.
4. Stir butter until it foams and turns to a deep amber brown color.
5. Add the onions and garlic, remove from heat then scrape into a mixing bowl.
6. Add remaining ingredients, except pumpkin and water, to the bowl; stir well.
7. Fill the pumpkin with the mixture to the top then cover with pumpkin top.
8. Make a foil sling for the pumpkin (see page 8).
9. Pour the water into the pressure cooker then lower the pumpkin into the pressure cooker using the foil sling; secure lid.
10. Set steam vent to **SEAL** and timer to 25 minutes.
11. When cooking is complete, let pressure release naturally (about 10 minutes).
12. Remove lid then carefully remove the pumpkin by the foil sling.
13. Slice pumpkin into wedges before serving.

ENTREES

QUINOA
PILAF

Makes 6 servings

For the Quinoa:

2 cups quinoa
2 1/2 cups water
1 tablespoon powdered chicken bouillon, such as Maggi
1 tablespoon soy sauce
2 tablespoons olive oil
1/2 teaspoon dried thyme
1 small yellow onion, diced
1 cup sliced almonds, toasted
1 cup raisins
1/2 cup dried apricots, diced
1/2 teaspoon chili flakes, or to taste

For Finishing:

1 bunch green onions, sliced
1 cup red grapes, halved
2 tablespoons fresh parsley, chopped
Zest and juice of 1 lemon
Kosher salt and fresh pepper to taste

Method:

1. Using a fine strainer, rinse the quinoa for 1 minute to remove the bitter natural coating.
2. Place all quinoa ingredients into the pressure cooker; secure lid.
3. Set steam vent to **SEAL** and timer to 6 minutes.
4. When cooking is complete, let pressure release naturally (about 10 minutes).
5. Remove lid then add all finishing ingredients to the pressure cooker; stir.
6. Taste and adjust seasoning if desired.
7. Serve hot, at room temperature or cold (keeps well, covered and refrigerated for up to 5 days).

TIP

This is a very forgiving recipe so you can add or replace any ingredient you like.

SILKY FLAN WITH MICROWAVE CARAMEL

Makes 4 servings

Ingredients:

1 cup milk
1 cup heavy cream
2/3 cup sugar
1/8 teaspoon kosher salt
1 teaspoon pure vanilla extract
2 large eggs
3 large egg yolks
1 recipe microwave caramel (see recipe on page 105)
1 1/2 cups water

Method:

1. In a large bowl, combine all ingredients, except microwave caramel and water; whisk until completely combined.
2. Pour microwave caramel into a 7-inch cake pan or 3 mini cake pans then swirl to coat the bottom(s).
3. Pour mixture into the caramel-lined pan(s) then cover with aluminum foil.
4. Place a metal rack into the bottom of the pressure cooker.
5. Make a foil sling for the cake pan(s) (see page 8).
6. Pour the water into the pressure cooker then lower the cake pan(s) by the foil sling into the pressure cooker; secur
7. Set steam vent to **SEAL** and timer to 20 minutes.
8. When cooking is complete, let pressure release naturally (about 10 minutes).
9. Remove lid and let cool for 1 hour before removing the pan(s) by the foil sling.
10. Refrigerate covered for a minimum of 4 hours.
11. To serve, run a thin bladed knife around the edge of the pan(s) then invert onto a serving plate; gently tap the pan(s) to remove the flan(s).
12. Pour the now melted caramel in the bottom of the pan(s) over the dessert before serving.

OLD FASHIONED RICE PUDDING

Makes 4-6 servings

Ingredients:

1/2 cups long-grain white rice, uncooked
cup half & half
cups water
/4 cup sugar
/2 teaspoon kosher salt
teaspoons lemon juice
teaspoon vanilla extract
/4 teaspoon butter vanilla extract

Method:

1. Place all ingredients into the pressure cooker; stir then secure lid.
2. Set steam vent to **SEAL** and timer to 6 minutes.
3. When cooking is complete, let pressure release naturally (about 10 minutes).
4. Remove lid and stir pudding gently.
5. Garnish as desired and serve hot.

VANILLA BEAN
POACHED PEARS

Makes 6 servings

Ingredients:

6 firm Bosc pears, peeled with stems attached
1 1/2 cups granulated sugar
3 cups sweet white wine, such as Sauternes
1 cup water
1 vanilla bean, split
3-inch strip of peel from a lemon
3-inch strip of peel from an orange
The juice from the lemon and orange
2 cinnamon sticks

Method:

1. Place all ingredients into the pressure cooker; secure lid.
2. Set steam vent to **SEAL** and timer to 8 minutes.
3. When cooking is complete, let pressure release naturally (about 10 minutes).
4. Transfer pears to shallow serving bowls.
5. Pour desired amount of poaching liquid from the pressure cooker around each pear before serving.

TIP

If you need to avoid sugar, my favorite substitutes are Zsweet or agave syrup.

SOUR CREAM
COFFEE CAKE

Makes 1 cake

For the Batter:

cup unsalted butter
cup sugar
large egg
/2 cup sour cream
teaspoon vanilla extract
/4 teaspoon kosher salt
/2 teaspoon baking powder
cup all purpose flour, sifted

For the Filling/Topping:

1 cup brown sugar
2 teaspoons ground cinnamon
2 tablespoons all purpose flour

Method:

1. In a mixing bowl, beat together the butter and sugar using a hand mixer until fluffy.
2. Add the egg, sour cream and vanilla then mix until smooth.
3. Using low speed, stir in the salt, baking powder and flour until incorporated.
4. In a small bowl, stir together all filling/topping ingredients.
5. Apply nonstick spray to a cake pan that fits inside the pressure cooker.
6. Pour half of the batter into the cake pan then scatter half of the filling over the batter.
7. Top with remaining batter and remaining filling; cover with aluminum foil.
8. Place a metal rack into the bottom of the pressure cooker.
9. Make a foil sling for the cake pan (see page 8). (see page 8)
10. Pour 1 1/2 cups water into the pressure cooker then lower the pan into the pressure cooker using the foil sling; secure lid.
11. Set steam vent to **VENT** (not **SEAL** as you will not be cooking under pressure).
12. Set timer to 30 minutes and a separate kitchen timer to 30 minutes (setting the pressure cooker timer to 30 minutes will turn the cooker on but the timer will not count down because you are not cooking under pressure).
13. After 30 minutes of cooking, remove lid then remove pan by the foil sling.
14. Test for doneness by inserting a wooden toothpick off-center; it should come out with only a few moist crumbs clinging to it.
15. Let cool until warm then cut into squares before serving.

DESSERTS

PECAN BREAD PUDDING

Makes 3-4 servings

Ingredients:

4 cups croissants, cut into 1-inch cubes, lightly toasted
1/2 cup pecans, chopped
1 tablespoon unsalted butter, melted
2 large eggs, beaten
1/4 cup brown sugar
1/2 teaspoon cinnamon
1/2 teaspoon maple extract
1/4 teaspoon cider vinegar
1/4 teaspoon kosher salt
1 1/2 cups half & half
1 1/2 cups water

Method:

1. Lightly apply nonstick spray to an 8-inch cake pan or 3 baby cake pans that fit(s) inside the pressure cooker.
2. Place the croissants cubes into the cake pan(s).
3. In a large bowl, combine remaining ingredients, except water.
4. Pour mixture over the bread cubes in the cake pan(s) then cover tightly with aluminum foil.
5. Place a metal rack into the bottom of the pressure cooker.
6. Make a foil sling for the cake pan(s) (see page 8).
7. Pour the water into the pressure cooker then lower the cake pan(s) into the pressure cooker using the foil sling; secure lid.
8. Set steam vent to **SEAL** and timer to 15 minutes.
9. When cooking is complete, let pressure release naturally (about 10 minutes).
10. Remove lid and let cool for 30 minutes before removing the cake pan(s) by the foil sling.
11. Garnish as desired and serve.

DESSERTS

100

VANILLA WHITE CAKE

Makes 1 cake

Ingredients:

1/4 cup unsalted butter, softened
1/4 cup shortening
1 1/2 teaspoons baking powder
3/4 cup granulated sugar
1/2 teaspoon kosher salt
1 teaspoon vanilla extract
1/8 teaspoon almond extract
3 large egg whites
1 1/3 cups cake flour such as Swans Down, divided
1/2 cup whole milk, divided
1 1/2 cups water

Method:

1. Butter and flour a round cake pan that fits inside the pressure cooker; set aside.
2. In a bowl combine the butter, shortening, baking powder, sugar, salt and extracts; cream using a mixer for 5 minutes or until light and fluffy then scrape the sides.
3. Add the egg whites and beat well; scrape the sides.
4. Add 1/2 of the cake flour to the bowl, mix then add half of the milk and mix again; repeat with remaining cake flour and milk.
5. Pour batter into the prepared cake pan then cover with aluminum foil.
6. Place a metal rack into the bottom of the pressure cooker.
7. Make a foil sling for the cake pan (see page 8).
8. Pour the water into the pressure cooker then lower the cake pan into the pressure cooker using the foil sling; secure lid.
9. Set steam vent to **VENT** (not **SEAL** as you will not be cooking under pressure).
10. Set timer to 25 minutes and a separate kitchen timer to 25 minutes (setting the pressure cooker timer to 25 minutes will turn the cooker on but the timer will not count down because you are not cooking under pressure).
11. After 25 minutes of cooking, remove lid then test for doneness by inserting a wooden toothpick off-center; it should come out with just a few moist crumbs clinging to it.
12. Remove the pan by the foil sling then let cool until warm.
13. Garnish as desired before serving.

HOMEMADE
CHICKEN STOCK

Makes 6 cups

Ingredients:

2 1/2 pounds chicken parts, excluding breast meat
2 carrots, peeled and cut into 1-inch pieces
2 celery stalks, trimmed and cut into 1-inch pieces
1 medium yellow onion, unpeeled and quartered
6 whole peppercorns
8 cups water

Method:

1. Place all ingredients into the pressure cooker; secure lid.
2. Set steam vent to **SEAL** and timer to 45 minutes.
3. When cooking is complete, let pressure release naturally (about 10 minutes).
4. Carefully remove the pressure cooker insert from the pressure cooker and let cool for 30 minutes.
5. Place a large fine mesh strainer into a large bowl.
6. Pour mixture through the strainer into the bowl; discard chicken parts and vegetables.
7. Ladle the stock into containers then refrigerate until fat has solidified on the surface; remove the fat.
8. Stock can be refrigerated for up to 3 days or frozen for up to 3 months.

TIP

For brown chicken stock, roast the chicken parts in a 425°F oven for 45 minutes or until well browned before adding them to the pressure cooker. This extra step will give your chicken stock much more flavor.

EXTRAS

HOMEMADE
BEEF STOCK

Makes 6 cups

Ingredients:

3 pounds beef bones
2 large carrots, peeled and cut into 1-inch pieces
2 celery stalks, trimmed and cut into 1-inch pieces
1 large yellow onion, unpeeled and quartered
7 cups water
1 tablespoon tomato paste
6 whole peppercorns

Method:

1. Preheat oven to 425°F.
2. Place the bones, carrots, celery and onion into a roasting pan.
3. Put the pan in the oven and roast for 45 minutes then remove pan from oven.
4. Pour water into the pressure cooker.
5. Transfer the roasting pan contents and remaining ingredients to the pressure cooker; secure lid.
6. Set steam vent to **SEAL** and timer to 35 minutes.
7. When cooking is complete, let pressure release naturally (about 10 minutes).
8. Carefully remove the pressure cooker insert from the pressure cooker and let cool for 30 minutes.
9. Place a large fine mesh strainer into a large bowl.
10. Pour mixture through the strainer into the bowl; discard bones and vegetables.
11. Ladle the stock into containers then refrigerate until fat has solidified on the surface; remove the fat.
12. Stock can be refrigerated for up to 3 days or frozen for up to 3 months.

MAMA'S EASY
BOILED PEANUTS

Makes 2 pounds

Ingredients:

1 pound raw (dry) peanuts, in the shell
1/2 cup kosher salt or more if desired
5 cups water

Method:

1. Place all ingredients into the pressure cooker; secure lid.
2. Set steam vent to **SEAL** and timer to 90 minutes.
3. When cooking is complete, let pressure release naturally (about 10 minutes).
4. Let rest for 1 hour on **KEEP WARM**.
5. Reheat boiled peanuts in the microwave before serving.
6. Boiled peanuts will keep in the refrigerator for 7 days or in the freezer for up to 3 months.

TIP
You can change the flavor by adding chili flakes, garlic or vinegar in step 1.

MICROWAVE
CARAMEL

Ingredients:
2 cup sugar
4 cup corn syrup
drops fresh lemon juice

Method:

1. *Place all ingredients into a 2 or 4 cup glass measuring cup; stir until all of the sugar is moistened.*
2. *Microwave on high for about 3 minutes or until bubbles start piling up on top of each other and mixture starts turning amber in color (time may vary depending on your microwave).*
3. *Carefully remove from microwave and let rest for up to 30 seconds (color will deepen as it rests).*
4. *Use immediately before it hardens (use caution as caramel is very hot).*

TIP

This recipe is great for caramelized sugar on top of Crème Brûlée if you do not have a blow torch.

SOURCE PAGE

Here are some of my favorite places to find ingredients that are not readily available at grocery stores as well as kitchen tools and supplies that help you become a better cook.

The Bakers Catalogue at King Arthur Flour

135 Route 5 South
P.O. Box 1010
Norwich, VT 05055

Mini or baby cake pans, pure fruit oils including Fiori di Sicilia, citric acid, silicone spatulas, digital timers, silicone cupcake molds, off-set spatulas, measuring cups and spoons, blow torch, knives, ice cream scoops, microplane graters
www.kingarthurflour.com

Benton's Smoky Mountain Country Hams

2603 Highway 411
Madisonville, Tennessee 37354
423-442-5003

The best, smokiest bacon in the world
www.bentonshams.com

Chocosphere

P.O. Box 2237
Tualatin, OR 97062
877-992-4623

Excellent quality cocoa (Callebaut)
All Chocolates
Jimmies and sprinkles
www.chocosphere.com

www.cheftools.com

309 S. Cloverdale St. C35
Seattle, WA 98108
206-933-0700

Vast inventory of really cool chef-type stuff
www.cheftools.com

Anson Mills

1922-C Gervais St.
Columbia, SC 29201
803-467-4122

Amazing stone ground grits
www.ansonmills.com

Vanilla From Tahiti

Nui Enterprises
501 Chapala St. Suite A
Santa Barbara, CA 93101
805-965-5153

My favorite pure vanilla extract and the best quality vanilla beans I have ever used
www.vanillafromtahiti.com

Whole Foods

550 Bowie St.
Austin, TX 78703
512-477-4455

Large pearl tapioca, stone milled grits, citric acid, natural and organic products
www.wholefoods.com

Fortune Products Inc.

205 Hickory Creek Road
Marble Falls, TX 78654
830-693-6111

Hand-held, inexpensive Accusharp knife sharpeners
www.accusharp.com

D & G Occasions

625 Herndon Ave.
Orlando, FL 32803
407-894-4458

My favorite butter vanilla extract by Magic Line, cake and candy making supplies, citric acid, pure fruit oils, professional food colorings, ultra-thin flexible spatulas, large selection of sprinkles and jimmies, unusual birthday candles, pure vanilla extract, pastry bags and tips, parchment, CK Products
www.dandgoccasions.com

Penzeys Spices

P.O. Box 924
Brookfield, WI 53045
800-741-7787

Spices, file' powder, Creole seasonings, pimenton, extracts, seasonings and more
www.penzeys.com

Beans About Cooking

100 Indian Rocks Road North Suite G
Belleair Bluffs, FL 33770
727-588-3303

Cheesecloth, inexpensive "harp" shaped vegetable peelers, measuring cups and spoons, knives, vast array of kitchen tools including microplane graters, spiders, blow torch, English muffin molds, silicone cupcake molds, flexible spatulas
Beansaboutcooking@hotmail.com

INDEX

INDEX

FOR ALL OF MARIAN GETZ'S COOKBOOKS AS WELL AS
COOKWARE, APPLIANCES, CUTLERY AND KITCHEN ACCESSORIES
BY WOLFGANG PUCK

PLEASE VISIT HSN.COM
(KEYWORD: WOLFGANG PUCK)